Engaging the Hispanic Learner

Engaging the Hispanic Learner

Ten Strategies for Using Culture to Increase Achievement

Michele Wages, PhD

ROWMAN & LITTLEFIELD
Lanham • Boulder • New York • London

Published by Rowman & Littlefield
A wholly owned subsidiary of The Rowman & Littlefield Publishing Group, Inc.
4501 Forbes Boulevard, Suite 200, Lanham, Maryland 20706
www.rowman.com

Unit A, Whitacre Mews, 26-34 Stannary Street, London SE11 4AB

British Library Cataloguing in Publication Information Available

Library of Congress Cataloging-in-Publication Data

Wages, Michele, 1965–
Engaging the Hispanic learner : ten strategies for using culture to increase achievement / Michele Wages.
pages cm.
Includes bibliographical references.
ISBN 978-1-4758-1385-2 (cloth : alk. paper) — ISBN 978-1-4758-1386-9 (pbk. : alk. paper) — ISBN 978-1-4758-1387-6 (electronic)
1. Hispanic Americans—Education. 2. Hispanic Americans—Education—Social aspects. 3. Hispanic American students—Social conditions. 4. Educational anthropology—United States. 5. Community and school—United States. I. Title.
LC2669.W34 2014
371.829'68073—dc23
2014029860

Do you need help in identifying how culture is affecting your Hispanic students' educational success? Within the pages of this book you will discover ten effective instructional strategies along with numerous examples based on Hispanic cultural perceptions of education. Each chapter is self-sufficient, allowing the reader to utilize only those parts of the book needed. This is an invaluable educator resource addressing the increasingly diverse student population in today's classroom.

—Michele Wages

Contents

Foreword

What can I do differently, to better help my Hispanic students?

This is one of the fundamental questions every teacher must now ask, every year, as a new group of students walks through the classroom door. The reason, quite simply, is that the percentage of Hispanic students in US classrooms is increasing dramatically each year. As educators, what should we do, what should we change, what should we try, that might better help these students maximize their potential?

In the past, education's overall approach was to let Hispanic learners simply adapt to the typical US, anglo-dominated classroom culture. The expectation was they would acclimate themselves to the current norms. In fact, it was almost as if there was an unspoken rule that it was the *student's responsibility* to figure out how to fit in. If, arguably, that indeed was the situation, it is certainly no longer true. Given the seismic shift in percentages, it's time for schools and teachers to proactively develop learning environments that will support these students in the best possible way.

For many teachers, this is not news. They've seen the growing need for a response to the changing dynamics of classroom populations over the last few years. In my experience, however, what has been lacking are specific strategies we can implement to properly address the situation. While identifying the issue and seeing the need for change are both important, the next step is knowing what to do—and doing it.

In *Engaging the Hispanic Learner,* Michele Wages helps education take an enormous step forward in addressing this increasingly complex issue. The research she cites is almost shockingly compelling. After reading this book there should be no doubt in anyone's mind that the issue is real, the issue is important, and that successfully dealing with it—soon—is critical.

Perhaps most importantly, she offers us specific things we can do to better meet this challenge. The ten strategies she offers are practical, applicable, and achievable. When successfully applied they will work together to produce a better result than any one alone might create.

However, with that being said, for those short on time, the good news is that you don't have to read it all. One of the wonderful things about *Engaging the Hispanic Learner* is that you don't have to read far before the vital, practical pieces of the puzzle start to fall into place. Just by dipping anywhere into the book, teachers will be able to begin implementing Michele Wages' ideas immediately. This makes the book a highly valuable resource for busy teachers, who can look at almost any section and within a few minutes select an idea, a tool, or a strategy, and put it into action the next day.

Some people will likely see the issue of addressing the needs of Hispanic learners as a lesser problem than other issues we are currently facing in education. Yet perhaps the more useful thought would be to see it as the tremendous opportunity it truly is. These students are going to be an important part of our country's—and indeed the world's—future. The sooner we address the situation, the sooner they can and will become positive, powerful, and productive contributors to society.

The time is certainly right for education to step up and take charge of this critical situation. It's time for us to reach out and lend a hand where it's greatly needed—to help these students who so desperately need our assistance. It's time for us to switch from passive response mode into proactive action mode, and make some real changes for the better.

In *Engaging the Hispanic Learner*, Michele Wages has given us an important, practical starting point from which we can begin this essential journey.

—Dr. Rich Allen

Preface

The census bureau has predicted that by the year 2100, the minority will become the majority, with non-Hispanic whites comprising only 40 percent of the US population (Noor, 2012). According to the National Center for Educational Statistics (NCES) 2011, "Black and Hispanic youth are more likely than whites or Asians to drop out of high school."

In 2012, 4 percent of anglo students ages sixteen to twenty-four were not enrolled in school and had not completed high school, compared with 9 percent of blacks and 13 percent of Hispanics. The high rate for Hispanics not completing school is partly due to the high proportion of immigrants in this age group who never attended school in the US. Also included in this report was the fact that the higher dropout rate existed among Hispanics who were foreign born (31 percent) versus those who were native born (10 percent), which partially accounts for the relatively high overall Hispanic dropout rate of 16 percent.

Costantini (2012) found that Hispanic students were less likely to graduate from high school than whites and Asians in all but two states over the 2010–2011 school year. Those two states, Maine and Hawaii, showed Hispanic graduation rates slightly higher than those of their white peers. "Approximately 42 percent of Hispanic students, 43 percent of African American, and 46 percent of American Indian students will not graduate on time with a regular diploma, compared to 17 percent of Asian students and 22 percent of white students (Alliance for Excellent Education" (AEE, 2011). "Nationally, of the 71 percent of all students that graduate from high school on time, less than half of Hispanic students earn diplomas with their peers" (Virginia Department of Education, 2009).

According to a study conducted by the Migration Policy Institute (2011), there are three main reasons Hispanics drop out of school:

1. *Legal status.* Because more than seven in ten Hispanics are unauthorized and thus, ineligible for employment and most educational aid.

2. *Low English skills*. More than half of Hispanics have extremely poor understanding and use of the English language (i.e., they reported speaking English "not well" or "not at all"). For Latino youth in particular, the majority are recent immigrants who are English-language learners or second language acquisition students. This fact increases the risk of these students dropping out or not completing high school on time (Fry, 2003).

3. *Low education*. Due to many Hispanics coming to the US for work, they have limited or interrupted education in their home countries. As time passes, this gap in education becomes larger, and fewer opportunities exist for these young adults to recover education.

According to the National Center for Educational Statistics (NCES, 2011), "from 28 to 40 percent of Hispanic children from Mexico enrolled in public grade school are enrolled at a grade level below normal for their age, compared to 20 to 25 percent of non-Hispanic white children." A more shocking statistic in this same report is that "Hispanic students in grades 4 and 8 performed below their white classmates by an average of more than 20 points on reading assessments" (NCES, 2011). This 20-point difference equals an achievement difference of approximately two grade levels (NCES, 2011).

In addition, an article by DeRuy (2012), states that "fourth grade Latinos scored above the international average for most measures on the international tests, but the eight-grade Latino students did not." The American Psychological Association (2012) claims "there is no single prominent risk factor predicting dropout. Rather there are numerous risk factors that in combination with each other raise the probability of youth leaving high school early" (Dynarski & Gleason, 2002). These factors fall into four broad categories related to *individuals* (e.g., truancy, poor school attitude), *families* (e.g., low-income, lack of parental involvement), *schools* (e.g., negative school climate, low expectations), and *communities* (e.g., high crime, lack of community support for schools), according to the Center for Mental Health in Schools, UCLA (2007).

Statistically, dropout rates particularly correlate with high poverty rates, poor school attendance, poor academic performance, grade retention (i.e., being held back), and disengagement from school (Hammond, Linton, Smink & Drew, 2007). Fortunately, there is an increase in the amount of research for schools on how to prevent dropping out by addressing core factors such as problem behaviors, promoting academic success, and enhancing overall health and well-being for students.

The question in today's schools is not which bilingual program works, but how today's educators can use their understanding of the Hispanic culture to motivate students and increase achievement and success. "For it is not the students' job to change their lives to make their school work better. It is up to schools to adapt to work better for students" (Jensen, 2013).

Introduction

With an estimate of more than 50 million Hispanics in the United States, they are the fastest growing demographic, but have performed at some of the lowest educational success rates (U.S. Department of Education; White House Initiative, 2011). This steadily growing number has resulted in 12.4 million Hispanic students being enrolled in K-12 public schools. This means that in today's classrooms 1 in 5 American students are of Hispanic descent. There is an educational crisis facing the Hispanic students in today's classrooms.

One of the most alarming facts is that many Hispanics do not even enter high school and many of these students live in households and communities that experience high and sustained rates of poverty. A 2005 United Nations report found that the United States had the highest rate of child poverty among all twenty-four Organization for Economic and Cooperative Development (OECD) countries, exceeded only by Mexico (UNICEF, 2005). Some educators have argued that one of the most serious barriers to achievement among Hispanic students is the more rigorous curricula, as well as the fact that disadvantaged students are often not expected to perform as well (Webley, 2011).

Other studies suggest this is not the case, but the "reality of it is, as public educators, we need to educate whoever comes through the door. So if 35 percent of your students are Hispanic, you have to address their needs" (Webley, 2011). A study by Menken and Holmes (2000), showed three main factors affecting Hispanic student success in today's public schools: inadequate preparation among teachers, ineffective teaching practices, and at-risk school environments.

Inadequate Preparation among Credentialed Teachers

Schools require many resources to function well. One important resource is highly qualified personnel. Today's overwhelmingly white

1

teaching force has little preparation or training to deal with the demographic changes appearing in our classrooms, including the contributions and cultures of other groups in the society (Frankenberg & Siegel-Hawley, 2008). "Currently, more than one out of four of all children from the United States are from immigrant families. In Texas, 15 percent of the total public school population are ELLs" (Center for American Progress, 2012).

The disconnect is in the fact that few of the teachers are prepared to teach Hispanic ELLs even though statistics show the overwhelming need for such teachers. There has also been little attention paid to the essential standards, knowledge, and skills that today's teachers ought to possess in order to provide effective instruction to ELLs placed in their classrooms (Samson & Collins, 2012). "Teachers of ELL students need the appropriate training to be able to meet their students' language and learning needs and to facilitate academic growth, yet most teachers lack this training" (Gandara, Maxwell-Jolly, & Driscoll, 2005).

Ortiz (2001) believes that there must be a common philosophy shared by all teachers which includes a knowledge base relative to the education of students learning English. This knowledge base should include: the understanding of second language acquisition; how to assess the student's proficiency in their native language and English/academic language; how sociocultural influences affect learning; what strategies are effective for first and second language instruction; various informal assessment strategies that can assist in monitoring progress, particularly in language and literacy development; and effective instructional strategies for successfully working with culturally and linguistically diverse families and communities (Ortiz, 2001).

Ineffective Teaching Practices

In today's classrooms, the predominantly used instructional approach has exposed a second problem related to Hispanic failure. In many schools that serve Hispanic students, more than 80 percent of US teachers are white and 75 percent of these are female (U.S. Census Bureau, 2006). Because of these high anglo percentiles in the schools' teaching force, classrooms are places that exemplify white norms and middle-class values (Thompson, 2001). This has resulted in a vast difference between the student body and the teaching force, causing many Hispanic students to go through school without ever having someone at the front of the class who reflects their race or culture (Irvine, 2003).

University programs are not properly preparing teachers, leaving the future workforce unfamiliar with cultural diversity and various strategies and approaches to address them. This lack of preparation causes the anglo teacher to refer back to how they were taught, which for the majority was a teacher-centered classroom. This teacher-directed approach emphasizes lecture and "drill and kill," and centers around student seatwork involving a multitude of worksheets (Stephen, Varble, & Taitt, 1993). The result of this lack of training is teachers holding lower expectations for the academic achievement of ELLs, which in turn causes more time to be spent explaining things to students than questioning, cuing, or prompting them to respond (Ruiz-de-Velasco & Fix, 2001).

Instead of developing students' capacity to read, discuss, and write substantive texts in multiple genres (Langer, 2002; Schleppegrell, 2002), teachers typically implement their own type of modification for linguistic needs of students by taking a reductive approach of simplified content and a focus on isolated basic skills (MetLife, 2001). Rist (1973) noted that students whose teacher held lower expectations were called on less in class, received far less positive feedback, and received less direct instruction and interaction with the teacher (Rist, 1973). Today's schools are a far cry from the quality of instruction required for the diversity of our classrooms (Cheung and Slavin, 2005). Wiggins, Follo, & Eberly (2007) state that "understanding a community and having a positive attitude toward cultural diversity are critical components in the preparation of teachers, but few universities provide exposure to effective practices and training to potential teachers."

At-Risk School Environment

The last factor actually combines the first two. By attending schools that are poorly maintained along with having teachers that are not qualified, Hispanic students are learning in a school environment that qualifies as at-risk. "Hispanic students who attend these at-risk schools merit our special attention, because if we can alter their learning environment, it may be possible to improve both their education and their overall chances for success in society" (Waxman, 1992).

According to the 2000 Census, the median annual household income for Hispanics was $33,000, compared with $47,000 for anglos. It is common knowledge that students from lower socioeconomic backgrounds may have difficulty if instruction presumes middle-class experiences (Jensen, 2013). It is truly unfortunate, however, that the most at-risk schools with the highest number of minority students and the lowest-income student population usually have the least experienced and least qualified teachers.

Failure to address the needs of high-risk students can lead to them dropping out of high school, which often results in negative employment and life outcomes. When a student drops out of high school they are unlikely to have the minimum skills and credentials necessary to function in today's increasingly complex society and technology-dependent workplace. The minimum requirement in today's job market or in continuing into higher education is the completion of high school (Laird, Lew, & Chapman, 2006).

Having a high school diploma is associated with higher incomes and occupational status (Chen & Kaplan, 2003), and "those young adults with low education and skill levels are more likely to live in poverty and to receive government assistance" (Laird, Kienzel, DeBell, & Chapman, 2007). "High school dropouts are also more likely to become involved in crime" (Lochner & Moretti, 2004), and many with the dropout status have been linked with poor health, including poor mental health (Alliance for Excellent Education, 2006). Such negative outcomes, along with diminished labor force participation, exact a high economic toll on society. "If the dropouts from the nation's class of 2011 had graduated, the US economy would benefit by about $154 billion dollars over their lifetimes" (Alliance for Excellent Education, 2011).

Many professionals have maintained that providing students with better teachers and classroom instruction is the best way to improve the education of Hispanic children (Tharp, Estrada, Dalton, & Yamauchi, 2000). It is also widely accepted that the home environment contributes significantly to student achievement in schools. If a mismatch exists between school and home environments, this can have a significant influence on achievement. Lack of social or cultural capital—the various linguistic and cultural competencies that schools require for educational success—are often attributed to the mismatch. However, these competencies are not explicitly taught in school, and children may or may not acquire these skills at home.

Recent encouraging research has found that good parenting practices have not only facilitated learning in the elementary setting, but have resulted in strong social skills for young Latino children in low-income areas. "However, these gains are undermined by mediocre schools as they grow older" (Fuller & Coll, 2010). Few researchers or educators speak of how students from Mexico have experiences, family backgrounds, and expectations that conflict with the expectations of the American classroom environment. By understanding these differences, teachers can help Hispanic students and their parents succeed. This book examines effective teaching practices to better understand student culture, and provides easy-to-implement instructional activities that help Hispanic students succeed.

THE FACTS

Why Students May Feel Uncomfortable

The family is the center of the social life in the Hispanic culture. This means that many children have not had much exposure to others outside their extended families. Most students from Mexico may have grown up only playing with siblings and cousins. When these students enter an American classroom, it is often the first time they have been exposed to an environment with varying types of people. Along with this, it may also be the first time the Hispanic student has been surrounded by different culture, language, food, and expectations. Without assistance from the teacher in understanding these differences, a student could fall into a pattern of social isolation and low educational achievement (Gandora, 2010).

Public Education System in Mexico

The Secretariat of Public Education (SEP) is responsible for the content of the national curriculum, while the National Institute for Assessment of Education (NIAE) monitors standards in schools. The national curriculum, followed in both the public and private sector, is broad-based and includes Spanish, mathematics, natural sciences, history, geography, civic education, art, and physical education (Clark, 2013). Proof of Mexican citizenship is required to attend public schools for free, which includes compulsory education PreK-9th grade. Because of poverty problems in

Mexico, only a small percentage (5 percent) of the annual financial plan is reserved for education.

Although K–12 schools promise free education, students are required to buy their own textbooks after the initial six years of grade school. The school libraries are devoid of fiction literature, and due to the limited supplies of books, students and teachers use them only on-site. Most young children attend primary school but only 62 percent reach secondary school. Of that 62 percent, around 45 percent of Mexican students finish secondary school. High school is not mandatory. Students that are enrolled can either receive a vocational certificate or get a diploma to then move to a four-year university to receive a degree.

The normal size for a preschool class in Mexico is 35–50 students and is required for all children ages three to five. The third year of preschool is equal to kindergarten in the United States. Upon completion of pre-school, students receive a graduation document which is required before entering primary school. Primary school has three sessions:

- Morning session: 8:00 a.m. until 12:00 p.m.
- Afternoon session: 2:00 p.m. until 6:00 p.m.
- Evening session: 7:00 p.m. until 9:00 p.m.

Each session is operated as a separate school. The same or some of the same educators may serve as the principal or faculty members in more than one session. In mountainous rural areas, cold mornings may prompt a much later starting time, and there usually is only one session in more remote places. Students generally study Spanish and mathematics at the beginning of the school day.

Students do not change classes; rather, the teachers rotate and there are no lockers, which requires students to carry all their materials throughout the day. During the first two grades, 45 percent of class time is devoted to Spanish. The school day includes a recess, during which students may play in the patio area and eat a snack. Children bring something from home or buy food such as eggs, French fries, ice cream, or fruit from the school. There is no designated eating area on the school campus. Recess is unsupervised, leaving students to resolve issues as they arise.

The school year in Mexico is based on the National School Calendar of two hundred days (August through July). The majority of schools in Mexico use a 10-point grading system, with 10 the maximum grade. Passing grades are from 6.0 to 10; 5.9 and below is not a passing grade. Report cards go home five times a year; in addition to at least a 6.0 score, students must have 80 percent attendance to be promoted.

Parents' Expectation for Education

According to Stein (2004), parents from Mexico have a very comprehensive definition of what makes a good education. The broad education of a child is what is important, rather than solely the formal schooling of a child. To most Hispanic parents, a sense of moral and personal responsibility serves as the foundation of a good education. In Mexico, this includes teaching a child how to treat elders with respect, behave properly, and become a person of good moral standing. "Many families still consider education only important through the primaria years (K-6) and there is significant attrition after 6th grade in urban as well as rural schools" (Stein, 2004).

Education and learning has a high value for parents in Mexico, but an understanding that schooling is the responsibility of the teacher and the school rather than the parents exists. Most parents are not aware that in America, children enter kindergarten already knowing their ABCs, colors, and numbers. Many Hispanic parents might expect that their son or daughter would learn these things in school. In Mexico, parents are invited to school with the expectation of monetary support or in-kind support (painting the school, cleaning the schoolyard, providing food for an event), but parent involvement in education is not required or even encouraged in public schools.

Teachers need to also realize that many new immigrant parents work long hours, may be unable to read, or may have household needs other than books or school supplies. Stein (2004) states that "in Mexico, teachers are responsible for the students' education. Parents are not expected to help with homework." However, parents attend regular meetings often focused on fundraising and support for the school. Attendance for these meetings is usually good because fines are assessed or report cards withheld when parents do not attend. Since schooling is viewed as the responsibility of the teacher, Hispanic parents may not understand that the teachers' request to bring in supplies are to be followed, that open houses are normally attended by parents, or that homework is often completed before family time in the average American household.

"One of the most important factors in school success is the extent to which parents actively participate in their children's education prior to their entry into formal preschool or kindergarten programs" (U.S. Department of Education, 2003). To enhance children's language acquisition, early reading performance, social development, and eventual success in school, specific activities can be used (Loeb, Fuller, Kagan, and Carrol, 2004). When the only or the predominant language spoken at home is Spanish, in addition to living in disadvantaged communities, the American culture and education practices take a backseat to trying to make ends meet while dealing with lower levels of education and less income. This has a drastic effect on young children in the household who are preparing to enter school (National Research Council, 2006).

Behavior Norms

Each student in a classroom brings his or her own set of behavior norms from home, and Hispanic students are no exception. In the case of parents who are from Mexico, their children show respect by not bothering or interrupting adults, not acting out in public, and quickly complying to an elder's request. To these parents, respecting a teacher means refraining from acting silly or calling out, or not asking questions if they feel it would be bothering the teacher. Hispanic students may approach the teacher quietly and wait to be acknowledged before asking their question.

Being or performing in front of the class may feel uncomfortable for some Hispanic students. This is due to Mexico schools not commonly encouraging students to show off their knowledge, nor rewarding them for doing so. Modesty prevents Hispanic students from getting pleasure when performing in front of others or displaying information upon request. Fortunately, these students thrive in small-group settings; as a classroom teacher, one needs to be aware of this.

Poverty's Role in Education

The largest group of children living in poverty is from the Hispanic culture. PEW Hispanic Center (2011) stated that "6.1 million Hispanic children are poor compared with 5 million non-Hispanic white children and 4.4 million black children." PEW goes on to state that poverty numbers in the Hispanic culture have soared in recent years due to the impact of recession on Latinos. It may be surprising to know that native-born Hispanics, for the most part, have lower poverty rates than do foreign-born Hispanics. This is due primarily to native Hispanics benefitting from having more education, better English fluency, and being US citizens by birth. In 2009, "over one third of all Hispanic children were living in poor families and the poverty rate was even higher (almost 40 percent) among foreign born Hispanic children" (Orrenius & Zavodny, 2011). Sources have shown that the highest poverty rates exist among immigrants from Mexico and the Caribbean.

The poverty gap in the Hispanic community is caused by lower educational attainment; in other words, the larger the difference in the average education level among household heads, the greater the gap. This gap boosts the poverty rate upward 1.2 percent among all Hispanics with the most important impact factor being the limited ability to speak English. Sosnowski (2010) reported that in 2010, "32.3 percent of Hispanic children in the US lived in poverty. Poverty also affects student brain development, relationships with peers, and the ability to complete a formal education. More than 1/3 of low income students begin kindergarten not ready for school."

ONE

Strategy 1: Culturally Responsive Teaching

Teachers need to connect the child's life experiences and interests to the existing curriculum.
—John Dewey, 1899

WHAT: DEFINING THE STRATEGY

Culture is a broad and comprehensive concept. It is not only a learned system of knowledge, behaviors, attitudes, beliefs, values, and norms that is shared by a group of people (Smith 1966), but also includes how people think, what they do, and how they use things to sustain their lives. The unique nature of each culture is what creates cultural diversity (Beebe, Beebe, & Redmond, 2005). Lessons become more relevant and meaningful for Hispanic students when they are exposed to different culture and people thus helping to prepare them for meaningful social roles.

Schools can assist Hispanic students by sending home a strong message communicating that the family language and culture are valuable assets to be preserved as students learn English and new content is mastered. Although many teachers try to discourage students from using their primary language, allowing two or more students to speak in their native language can be an effective way to share content information and provides an important break from English, particularly for new arrivals. Culture plays a role not only in communicating and receiving informa-

11

tion, but in the development of the thinking process of groups and individuals. Culture is more important than the educational field has let on.

Gay (2000) defines culturally responsive teaching as "using the cultural knowledge, prior experiences, and performance styles of diverse students to make learning more appropriate and effective for them; it teaches to and through the strengths of these students." Gay (2000) also describes culturally responsive teaching as having these characteristics:

- It acknowledges the legitimacy of the cultural heritages of different ethnic groups, both as legacies that affect students' dispositions, attitudes, and approaches to learning and as worthy content to be taught in the formal curriculum.
- It builds bridges of meaningfulness between home and school experiences as well as between academic abstractions and lived sociocultural realities.
- It uses a wide variety of instructional strategies that are connected to different learning styles.
- It teaches students to know and praise their own and each other's cultural heritages.
- It incorporates multicultural information, resources, and materials in all the subjects and skills routinely taught in schools (p. 29).

The majority of classroom interaction is based on the cultural norm of the white or European American middle-class values. Today's Hispanic students also have cultural norms and values they bring into the classroom; these values may very often conflict with the teacher's expectations and educators must recognize this fact. In today's multicultural classrooms teachers must connect teaching content to the cultural backgrounds of these students.

Teaching that ignores the norms of behavior and communication that a student brings may provoke student resistance, whereas exercising responsive teaching methods would prompt student involvement. According to the research, teaching that ignores student norms of behavior and communication provokes student resistance, while teaching that is responsive prompts student involvement (Olneck, 1995).

Using a knowledge of students' culture emphasizes the everyday concerns of students and also works to incorporate these concerns into the curriculum. Schools need to help Hispanic students navigate the bridge between their home culture and that of the school if these students are to become high academic achievers. To do this, teachers and administrators must foster a positive educational climate that shows respect for the students, culture, language, and prior knowledge. Some of these elements include:

1. Improving the acquisition and retention of new knowledge by working from students' existing knowledge base.
2. Improving self-confidence and self-esteem by emphasizing existing knowledge.
3. Increasing the transfer of school-taught knowledge to real-life situations.
4. Exposing students to knowledge about other individuals or cultural groups (Rivera & Zehler, 1991).

WHY: THEORETICAL FRAMEWORK

- The major resistance to using cultural background in teaching comes from the teacher's discomfort, if not fear of, addressing issues such as race and racism in their course (Cochran-Smith, 2004).
- Unfortunately, most pre-service teachers lack the knowledge, skills, dispositions, and experiences needed to teach ethnically and linguistically diverse students Thompson, Schmidt, & Davis, 2003).
- In order to teach to the different learning styles of students, activities would reflect a variety of sensory opportunities-visual, auditory, tactile (Gay, 2000).
- "Culturally responsive teachers teach the whole child, recognizing not only the importance of academic achievement, but also the maintaining of cultural identity and heritage" (Gay, 2000).
- "Strong, continual engagement among diverse students requires a holistic approach—that is, an approach where the how, what, and why of teaching are unified and meaningful" (Ogbu, 1995).
- Most of today's teachers realize they must change the way they teach in order to reach all students (Tomlinson, 1995).
- "A common misconception about culturally responsive instruction is that teachers must teach the 'Asian way' or the 'Hispanic way' or the 'black way'" (Rajagopal, 2011).

HOW: INSTRUCTIONAL ACTIVITIES

- Invite families to school on special occasions just to visit. While the family learns about the school and its policies and expectations, teachers can become acquainted with the families.
- Request that students write a story or essay about their families. Be sure to emphasize including parents, grandparents, brothers and sisters, cousins, and other relatives living in the home. Keep an open mind, and remember the importance of the extended family. Tell students before they write the story whether or not their stories or essays will be shared with the class.
- Schedule individual meetings with Hispanic/Latino students to discuss their families, but be careful that students understand the purpose of these discussions. Allow and respect a learner's privacy.
- Research the cultural background of students' families, visit local community centers to find out about the cultural activities and beliefs of the students and to tour students' neighborhoods to identify local resources and "funds of knowledge" (Moll et al., 1992).
- Communicate clear expectations; be specific in what you expect students to know and to be able to do. Create an environment in which there is genuine respect for students and a belief in their capability by encouraging them to meet expectations for a particular task and offering praise when standards are met.
- Implement cooperative learning strategies, which help teachers vary instruction and reinforce what the student has learned. This needs to be the core of instruction, only assigning independent work after students are familiar with a concept. Some ideas include role playing, using research projects that focus on cultural issues or concepts, and variations as to how a student can complete an assignment. Cultural differences can be bridged through effective communication and showing how student differences can make for better learning.
- Periodically, have students generate lists of topics they are interested in studying; this allows students to choose their own reading material and promotes student engagement.
- Embrace culture when creating a classroom environment. Implement patterns of management familiar to students and allow them ample opportunities to share about their culture.

- Utilize learning activities that are reflective of students' backgrounds. Cooperative learning is a key factor in this, which allows students a choice of working alone or in a group.
- Include resources from the students' community in order to better accommodate for diverse learning styles and language proficiency. This can include having members of the community mentor, teach a lesson, or speak about various subjects. Don't forget to invite parents or use them as presenters as well.

REFLECTION AND APPLICATION

1. How do school staff learn about the cultural norms and family histories that influence students' learning and behavior in school?

2. How often are stories from students' own lives and those of professional authors shared?

3. Are culturally meaningful instructional materials, such as print material in Spanish and print media written by and about Hispanic peoples, used in instruction? How often?

4. Are learning activities connected to students' family and community experience?

Modified from B. Schmitz, "Transforming a Course," *Center for Instructional Development and Research Teaching and Learning Bulletin* 2(4), 1–2.

TWO

Strategy 2: Second Language Acquisition

From whatever angle we look at it, bilingualism is a relative concept.
—Hoffman, 1991, p. 31

WHAT: DEFINING THE STRATEGY

As revealed in the introduction of this book, students that are ELLs constitute a significant percentage of the population of our nation's schools. "This population continues to increase more rapidly than that of native English speaking students" (Shore, 2001). The language minority population also has a high dropout rate. In addition, "these students are among the lowest ranking in academic achievement and expectations. They represent an at-risk population faced with a wide range of challenges" (Thompson, 2000).

It is in these challenges that today's teachers find themselves striving to help these students achieve in learning the English language and the academic material specified in content area learning standards. As educators, we must understand that each teacher, regardless of subject matter, that teaches in English to ESL students is not only a teacher of the content area but also a teacher of English as well.

With today's high-stakes testing, teachers must continually assess and reflect upon their teaching and update their practice to address the needs of this population, placing a stronger emphasis on the teaching of humans and less on that of a standardized test. Finding effective ways to present and enhance Hispanic student learning needs to be the continual focus in today's schools.

Second language acquisition is the process by which people learn a second language after a first language is already established. In the United States, second language learners are also known as ELLs (English Language Learners). Approximately 67 percent of ELLs are in the elementary school setting (Kindler, 2002), and the vast majority of ELLs speak Spanish (79.2 percent) as their first language (Kindler, 2002). Another interesting fact is that approximately two out of every three ELLs reside in five states: California, Texas, New York, Florida, and Illinois. "Despite this concentration of ELLs in specific states, virtually all states in the U.S. have seen a dramatic increase in their ELL population since 1990" (August & Shanahan, 2006).

There are hundreds of theorists whose strategies can be used by a teacher to create classroom conditions that foster learning by modeling, scaffolding, and helping students to construct understanding, with the eventual goal of becoming independent thinkers and problem solvers. Creating language-rich classrooms which provide students with advance organizers such as labeling everything in the classroom will build vocabulary and help students make connections to their native language through a multitude of media available for today's student use. Smartboards, slates, ELMO cameras, websites, and educational videos are just some examples of varying media.

WHY: THEORETICAL FRAMEWORK

- Teachers need to have an understanding of second language acquisition to better serve the culturally and linguistically diverse students in today's classrooms (Fillmore & Snow, 2002; Hamayan, 1990).
- Years of research in many fields including linguistics, psychology, sociology, anthropology, and neurolinguistics have been conducted to develop current theories of second language acquisition (Freeman & Freeman, 2001).
- Facial expression, voice tone, body gestures, and overall posture can make up to 92 percent of the communication in a message; as little as 7 percent may be expressed in words (McGee, 2012).

- In the not-so-distant past, deprivation in the home environment was considered the main cause of inferior academic achievement (Schneider & Lee, 1990).
- "By focusing on cultural-historical context, researchers have shifted to a more positive interpretation of the home environment, taking into account the funds of knowledge—the collective knowledge found among social networks of households that thrive through reciprocal exchange of resources" (Gonzalez et al., 1993) that are available within the students' home and community.

HOW: INSTRUCTIONAL ACTIVITIES

Listening

To build the skill of listening, the teacher can:

- *Use target terms:* Write down target terms, and when speaking, do so slowly and distinctly. When teachers speak, they are most likely unaware of how fast they go. A second language acquisition learner needs time to process what was said and translate it into his or her native language.
- *Use closed captioning:* Today's videos have closed captioning capabilities. This is excellent for the Hispanic students who can see words on the screen as the actors are speaking. Correlating written and spoken English helps the ELL student see spelling and sentence construction as well.

Visualization

Visualization is a term which represents the ability for students to take what they hear and create pictures in their head. This method strengthens reading comprehension and allows for more understanding of the text to be gained by the student. To do this, teachers can:

- Target visual literacy. Separate of language, visual literacy involves the ability to evaluate, apply or create conceptual visual representations. This makes it an invaluable tool for Hispanic Ell students to learn content and English simultaneously. This can be done when the teacher chooses to start with a short passage taken from a familiar text. Once the student listens to or reads several sentences few times, they can discuss the mental images that are forming in their heads.

- Choose text that is at the appropriate reading level, while equivalent in content and student interest for their age. Other programs include reading assessments to measure and track a student's reading level. One of the advantages in using these programs is that the student can often guess the meanings of unfamiliar words by looking at the illustrations resulting in less time being spent looking up new words in dictionaries.

  This method can also be used in group activities using a picture book and only sharing portions of the illustration, while asking students to finish the picture based on the text the teacher read. For ELLs, illustrations or comics provide an excellent supplement to literacy development.

- Use graphic organizers/charts, graphs and figures. These can be used at all grade and English proficiency levels. Graphic organizers provide visuals which assist students in the abstract thinking required when organizing text in order to understand it. The limited English proficiency of the ELLs often prevents them from being able to absorb the entire amount of content knowledge that native English-speaking students can absorb.

  Graphic organizers assist ELLs by providing a way to separate large amounts of content information into manageable chunks of information. Meaningful learning is introduced and encouraged for the ELL when charts, graphs, and figures are used to assess concepts and create relationships between new and learned information. ELLs can use graphic organizers to build their English skills, build background knowledge, and increase understanding, making learning more interesting and relevant.

Understanding Instruction

Second language acquisition takes time and the most successful program models include strategies that promote academic achievement and enable students to continue to develop academic skills along with learning a new language. Teachers need to understand that to develop ELLs' language skills they need to teach content along with increasing language skills. The following strategies can be helpful:

- Longer wait time: On average, the wait time in US classrooms is insufficient. To avoid an uncomfortable silence, a teacher may call on students that they know will provide the right answer. As the ELL student tries to translate terms and formulate explanations, this can short-circuit their thought process. Thus, developing a sufficient wait time is highly important.

  The effective teacher waits twenty seconds or more for a student to respond, but for many English Language Learners, even more time is needed to formulate answers. One approach is to have students work in pairs and reply to each other or write down responses and confirm them with the teacher. The teacher should always remember to allow the student to completely share his or her responses without interruption.

- Analogies: Whereas metaphors and similes are figure of speech, an analogy is a logical argument as to why two things are similar. When one presents an analogy, they may point out that two things being compared are alike by sharing characteristics.

  ELLs benefit from this strategy because it provides them with a way to relate new concepts to ones previously learned. ELLs can better understand and communicate complex relationships with limited language. Cognitive flexibility is promoted when they can discover that a concept can be represented in more than one type of relationship. In this way, new, unfamiliar learning can be connected and taught using familiar context.

Building Vocabulary

It is important for ELLs to build vocabulary over all school years. The teacher needs to select the key vocabulary in a concept. Here are some guidelines to help a teacher decide which words to tell and which words to teach an ELL student:

- *Tell* the word and move on if the word does not represent the taught concept or the student only needs the word for the present activity and will not likely use it again.
- *Teach* the word if it represents a new concept, has multiple meanings, or crosses content area. Some ideas of ways to teach new vocabulary to ELLs might include:

- Pronounce the word
- Provide a definition (show, paraphrase, act out, create experience)
- Post the definition for reference
- Introduce the word in the context in which it occurs or in a familiar context
- Relate the word to students' prior experiences; create an experience that demonstrates meaning
- Use word walls
- Generate and record sentences (building from original context or familiar context)
- Use the word often in instruction; point it out in other content areas; have students find it in other contexts, classes, out of school
- Add to word bank or student-made dictionaries
- Use first language to clarify
- Use word webs
- Use semantic-analysis charts or concept maps
- Act out the word using visuals or real objects

Using language-based games   There are two types of ELLs: native speakers and those pursuing English through bilingual instruction. Both methods can build up a student's skills, no matter their age or proficiency, by using games. The Internet is an infinite resource for vocabulary and concepts but usually requires minimal spoken language and a review of vocabulary.

Some great and useful games can be found at the following websites:

GameZone
Vocabulary.co.il
Power Words
LearnEnglish Kids
Funbrain Words
Vocabulary at ManyThings.org
ESL Fun Games Online
Dora's Alphabet Forest Adventure
EnglishClub ESL Games
Spelling & Word Relationships at Academic Skill Builders

Lord of the Flies
Word Games at Games for the Brain
Building Language for Literacy
Grammar Ninja
Word Games at Merriam-Webster
Language Arts Games at Mr. Nussbaum
Word Games at Pogo.com
Tracy Boyd's Quia
Grammar Practice Park
Literacy at BBC Schools
Reading Ring
ABC Order
Language Arts at iKnowthat.com
Power Proofreading
The ABC's Zoo Learning Game

Using a picture glossary or pictorial flashcards   In this approach, the term is written on one side of the card and a picture of the concept is on the other side, providing the Hispanic learner practice at correlating concepts directly with words and resulting in less transition being required.

A couple of Internet resources for ESL flashcards include:

http://esolhelp.com/esl-flashcards.html
http://havefunteaching.com/flash-cards/esl-and-esol-flash-cards/
www.english-4kids.com/flashcards.html

Flashcards are also a great tool for both cooperative and interactive learning. Here are some ideas:

Around the World: Competitive games help keep students engaged and motivated. Follow the basic directions for Around the World, but substitute vocabulary from content. These words can be put on flashcards to target learning.

Conversation starters: Another use of flashcards is to allow students to discuss and ask questions about pictures in small groups. Using this as a timed activity, pictures can be rotated around the class until all groups have seen all the pictures. The students can then discuss their views of what they saw and compare.

Memory: Have students match word to picture.

Writing prompts: Journals are a great tool. Give each student a picture and have them free-write or brainstorm about what they see.

Teaching root words   For an ELL student, an understanding of root words is extremely helpful. Prefixes, suffixes, and roots from Greek and Latin origins can greatly enhance student understanding of terms and facilitate a better use of the English language. Since approximately 50 percent of English words have Latin roots that are shared with the Spanish language, helping students make the connection is key. One helpful resource is www.learnthat.org/pages/view/roots.html.

Keeping cognates visible   Cognates are words that appear in two languages and share a similar meaning, spelling, and pronunciation. 30–40 percent of all words in English have a related word in Spanish. For the ELL student this presents a valuable bridge to the English language by linking English to what they already know. The following are some classroom strategies for teaching cognates:

1. *Read aloud:* When reading to students aloud, make a game out of having them raise their hands when they hear a cognate. Make a chart of the cognates and their meanings in both English and Spanish and post it in the classroom.

2. *Student reading*: Sticky notes have a great number of uses. Hand ELL students several, and as they read from the text, have them locate three or four cognates and write them down on the paper. After discussing their meaning, allow the students to add their sticky note to a larger poster posted in the room, keeping them as a visible resource.

3. *Follow-up activities*: In an activity known as Word Sort, a pair of students is given a set of cognates in which some are Spanish and some are English. Students take turns matching the Spanish to the English cognate. For more of a challenge, have the students turn all the cards face-down. They then take turns flipping two cards over: if they are a match, the student keeps the cards and goes again; if they do not match, the student turns the cards back over and their turn is over. The one with the most cards at the end wins.

Using mathematics translations   Today's educators face the challenge of bringing language and math instruction together. Even veteran teachers that have not taught content areas previously are being asked to lead and support instruction in the math classroom. Word problems are extremely difficult for ELLs, as translating common words to math symbols is exhausting for a second language acquisitioner. Brenda Krick-Morales writes, "Word problems in mathematics often pose a challenge because they require that students read and comprehend the text of the problem, identify the question that needs to be answered, and finally create and solve a numerical equation—ELLs who have had formal education in their home countries generally do not have mathematical difficulties; hence, their struggles begin when they encounter word problems in a second language that they have not yet mastered" (cited in Bernardo, 2005).

Here are some tips to increase student-to-student interaction with academic language in the math classroom:

- Let students work in pairs to translate symbols into words and write the sentence out. For example, $3x + 4 = 16$ would be written out "Three times x plus four equals sixteen." This allows students to process the information and the operations involved as they think through strategies to solve it. Students are also provided a chance to familiarize themselves with important vocabulary words.

- Post a visible word wall. Almost every classroom has a word wall of one design or another, which can take the form of a chart hung on the wall, words hanging from clothesline across the room, a bulletin board, or a personal list kept in the student's folder. Gradually adding words as the year passes allows the ELL student to build their vocabulary in small doses. Words should come from all content areas taught to assist in the understanding and comprehension of concepts. Pictures next to the word can also help students make connections and increase understanding.

REFLECTION AND APPLICATION

1. What curricular materials are needed for successful second language acquisition?

2. What type of instructional methods are needed to assist ELLs in language acquisition?

3. How do I promote a positive environment for ELLs which will motivate all students?

THREE

Strategy 3: Cooperative Learning

Coming together is a beginning; keeping together is progress; working together is success.
—Henry Ford

WHAT: DEFINING THE STRATEGY

When students actively work together in small groups to perform specific tasks, it is known as cooperative learning. Other names used include thematic instruction or integrated approach, but all are based on the focus that this approach is appropriate for all students, but is most critical for economically disadvantaged Hispanics (Padron, Waxman, & Rivera, 2002). The example of storytelling provides a wonderful vehicle to integrate English language learners into the classroom with the use of drawings and actions to support the stories they tell in either English or their native language.

Academic performance for Hispanic students has shown to improve through the use of cooperative learning activities by increasing motivation, strengthening self-esteem, encouraging student bonding, and promoting literacy skills. By creating more equitable groups and using activities that encourage individual student participation, teachers will see an increase in engagement of all students, but especially their Hispanic ones. Language skills are better developed because cooperative learning promotes peer interaction and the learning of concepts and content. One important factor when implementing cooperative learning is to assign

ELLs to different teams. These students will benefit from English being spoken by their peers and watching how other students express themselves when working in small teams.

WHY: THEORETICAL FRAMEWORK

One well-known fear teachers have about using cooperative learning is that low-status students will not participate and/or that high-status students will take over the group.

- For Hispanic students, cooperative learning is essential. In general, they do not openly wish to show what they know as it may embarrass others that do not know (McGee, 2012).
- When teaching the Hispanic student, teachers need to familiarize themselves with a variety of cooperative learning techniques such as creating equitable groups to enhance all student participation and multiple ability strategy implementation (Cohen, 1998) if cooperative learning is to work.
- There are three things teachers need to convince students of in the diverse classroom: "That different intellectual abilities are required in cooperative learning, that no one student has all the abilities needed, but that each member of the group will have some of the abilities" (Cohen, 1998).
- The influence of cooperative grouping on Hispanic students as an instructional practice are:
    1. Providing opportunities for students to communicate with each other.
    2. Enhancing instructional conversations.
    3. Decreasing anxiety.
    4. Developing social, academic, and communication skills.
    5. Boosting self-confidence and self-esteem through individual contributions and achievement of group goals.
    6. Improving individual and group relations by learning to clarify, assist and challenge others' ideas.
    7. Developing proficiency in English by providing students with rich language experiences that integrate speaking, listening, reading and writing (Calderon, 1991; Christian, 1995; Rivera & Zehler, 1991).

- Language opportunities are maximized and student comfort levels increased for ELL students when cooperative groups are used.
- The use of pre-teaching and scaffolding language for social skills benefits ELL students.
- Using cooperative activities that build upon student prior learning benefits ELLs by supporting practice with the target language.
- It is important to vary groups according to mastery of language acquisition. Using this method engages students to help each other complete assignments by rephrasing and reexamining information (Cohen, Lotan, & Holthuis, 1995).
- Group activities are dominant in the Hispanic culture. In groups, responsibility is shared and accountability is collective. The collectivistic culture emphasizes harmony and cooperation among the group (Gudykunst, 1998).

HOW: INSTRUCTIONAL ACTIVITIES

- Enhance previous learning by connecting the information from instruction through cooperative learning activities.
- Implement learned vocabulary and academic language into activities.
- Utilize activity formats and structures that are familiar to the students.
- Clearly identify goals and objectives and ensure that prerequisite skills are in place so authentic learning can take place.
- Remember that cooperative learning should not be overused, as these types of activities can be highly demanding linguistically. The general guideline is that ELLs should not work cooperatively for more than one-third of their academic tasks.
- Use instructional scaffolds such as vocabulary lists, sentence prompting, and repeated oral practice—these are successful strategies when the language proficiency levels of the students are also taken into account.
- Provide extended wait time during cooperative activities to allow for second language learners to process and formulate responses.
- Be sure to vary the size of groups for each activity. For more language support, move from pairs, to triads, to groups of four or five students.

- Keep in mind that language skills are a big factor when forming groups. Some parameters to factor in are familiarity with other students, language support, gender, and academic ability in relation to the proficiency levels of their ELL students.
- Use opportunities that vary purpose during group work. Some examples include practice and review, going deeper, narrowing content focus, and differentiation.
- Use homogenous grouping sparingly. Heterogeneous groups work most effectively, as ELL students benefit from the targeted instruction which this strategy provides; Hispanic students in particular need the rich language interaction they experience in mixed-level groups.
- Use role playing to share group management and leadership roles, placing an emphasis on equity and providing plenty of practice so all students are comfortable and understand the responsibilities of each role.
- Ensure that cooperative norms are taught and practiced—having norms in place results in students feeling respected and comfortable contributing at their level.
- Use a structured system to provide time for reflective processing in which all members get to share.
- Be specific when giving feedback. It must be clear and meaningful and targeted on areas such as how students honor the norms, play their roles, and contribute to the success of the group.

REFLECTION AND APPLICATION

1. How does classroom arrangement facilitate collaborative learning between students?

2. Is small group work structured so that students need to be concerned about the learning of all group members?

3. Does explicit collaboration skill instruction occur regularly, and do groups consistently process how effectively they work and learn together?

4. Are grouping practices organized in a variety of ways, including mixed academic achievement, interest, language, project, and friendship?

FOUR

Strategy 4: Cognitively Guided Instruction (CGI)

Teachers should assume that, like an iceberg that shows only a small amount of its mass above water, students have a great deal of competence that is not yet evident. Teachers need to be careful not to interpret silence or one-word answers as lack of knowledge.

—Mohr & Mohr, 2007, as cited in Cazden, 2001

WHAT: DEFINING THE STRATEGY

"Research has established that many teachers do not teach comprehension strategies to their students, thus creating a research to practice gap" (Pressley, 2006). To enhance students' metacognitive development, cognitively guided instruction method is essential. This method focuses on the direct teaching and modeling of cognitive learning, providing students with opportunities to practice them. Learning to monitor their own learning as a result of this explicit instruction helps students accelerate their acquisition of English and/or academic content (Waxman, Padron, & Knight, 1991). This instructional approach of cognitive strategies can remove some of the barriers to academic success for Hispanic students.

Based on the Iowa Core Curriculum for Mathematics at the elementary level, "Cognitively Guided Instruction (CGI) is a professional development program based on an integrated program of research focused on (a) the development of students' mathematical thinking; (b) instruction that influences that development; (c) teachers' knowledge and beliefs that

33

influence their instructional practices; and (d) the way that teachers' knowledge, beliefs, and practices are influenced by their understanding of students' mathematical thinking."

Students use procedures known as comprehension strategies to help them understand higher order tasks in reading (Paris, Lipson, & Wixson, 1994). Learning strategies that enhance students' metacognitive development is the emphasis of cognitive guided instruction with the main focus being that of direct teaching and modeling of cognitive learning strategies that accelerate ELL language acquisition and/or academic content. This trains students to monitor their own learning (Padron & Knight, 1989; Waxman, Padron, & Knight, 1991).

Listening to children's thinking and using it to create instruction is the primary practice of CGI. This allows an easier identification of what is difficult and what is easy for students to comprehend. The teacher can then focus our helping students build for future understanding based on their present knowledge while aiming to improve students' mathematical skills in the process.

Cognitive methods can be used to solve many types of problems, including number problems or editing a text for correct punctuation, both of which require the application of set rules. With the growing number of Hispanic students in today's classrooms, the barrier of the complex English language causes a struggle to develop higher-level reading and writing skills (Scarcella, 2002).

WHY: THEORETICAL FRAMEWORK

- Studies have consistently demonstrated that Cognitively Guided Instruction (CGI) students show significant gains in problem solving (Iowa Department of Education, 2013).
- The National Council of Supervisors of Mathematics (NCSM, 1977) and the National Council of Teachers of Mathematics (NCTM) 1980, 1989, and 2000, highly support the implementation of problem-solving at all grade levels.
- "The usefulness of dialogue with learners is well documented" (Buschman, 2001; Hoosain, 2000).
- Riordin and Noyce (2001), as well as Reyes, Scribner, and Scribner (1999), concluded that utilizing standards-based (usually problem-

based) curriculum results in children who do better on standard-ized tests than do those taught with other curriculums.

HOW: INSTRUCTIONAL ACTIVITIES

Cognitive Strategies Sentence Starters

The importance of students developing the procedural knowledge in how to implement strategies on their own, along with the conditional knowledge of why these strategies are useful, is key.

Metacognitive Reflections

Getting students to think about one's thinking is an essential strategic behavior. One idea is having the teacher talk aloud the process as they build an animal out of Play-Doh, recording the process as the animal is being built and students observe. Students then pair up and as one builds the animal, the other records his or her thought process.

Scaffolding Strategy Instruction

New skills are learned in context in which more skilled language us-ers are called upon to support others with unfamiliar tasks (Applebee & Langer, 1983, p. 168).

Color Coding

Many ELLs who have little practice think that the point of writing literary response-based analytical essays is to prove, by retelling the sto-ry, that they understood what they read. A deeper understanding is pos-sible if teachers use color coding, designating specific colors for the three types of assertions that make up an analytical essay. For example, Plot Summary is yellow (superficial and lightweight), Commentary is blue (goes beneath the surface), and Supporting Detail is green (gluing togeth-er plot summary and commentary).

Go through an essay together with the class so students can visually see the color patterns, then let students analyze samples of their own writing in pairs or in small groups.

REFLECTION AND APPLICATION

1. Does the teacher "think aloud" often to model metacognitive thinking for students?

2. Are students taught before-, during-, and after-reading strategies in all content areas to help them master academic material?

3. Is reciprocal teaching used in order to promote students' comprehension and monitoring their own thinking and learning?

4. Do teachers consistently model cognitive strategies and insist that students practice them until they can apply them in novel situations?

FIVE

Strategy 5: Instructional Conversations

Teachers that apply the concept of instructional conversations embrace the philosophy that talking and thinking go together and assume that the student may have something to say beyond what the student's teacher or peer is thinking or already knows.
—Mohr & Mohr, 2007

WHAT: DEFINING THE STRATEGY

Opportunities for conceptual and linguistic development can be created through discussion-based lessons known as instructional conversations. Meaning and relevance for students as well as concepts with educational value are the key focus to these conversations. The teacher's main role in an instructional conversation is what Perez (1996) calls conversational uptakes. These uptakes challenge the student and yet afford linguistic scaffolds to foster more in-depth discussion of academic topics. This is an opportunity for the teacher to encourage students' own ideas and build upon their experiences and ideas to guide them to higher levels of understanding. For ELLs, this provides the necessary interaction in social and academic situations at school and supplements the little interaction they receive from home.

Effective second language learning is best accomplished under conditions that "stimulate natural communicative interactions and minimize the formal instruction of linguistic structures, such as memorization drills and learning grammatical rules. An instructional conversation takes considerable knowledge of the subject matter under discussion and a great deal of planning before it can be carried out" (Goldenberg, 1991).

WHY: THEORETICAL FRAMEWORK

- Teachers rarely have the opportunity to participate on a regular basis in sustained conversations on academic topics with their students (Tharp & Dalton, 2007).
- An effective intervention for improving reading comprehension for ELLs is instructional conversation (IC). The IC approach has a demonstrated positive effect on ELL comprehension (U.S. Department of Education, 2006; Saunders, 1999; Saunders & Goldenberg, 1999).
- "From the early part of the 20th century up through today, researchers have promoted the value of discussions for developing critical thinking, productive social interaction, intellectual risk taking, and academic engagement" (Thayer, 1928; Wilen,1990).
- Teachers in general are motivated to conduct meaningful and productive discussions with students, but most are not properly trained and have few concrete models to do so (Saunders & Goldenberg, 1999).
- IC teachers talk significantly less than those using the direct lesson approach. The IC lesson is also more likely to be shaped and defined by mutual student and teacher understandings (Goldenberg & Patthey-Chavez, 1994).

HOW: INSTRUCTIONAL ACTIVITIES

Instructional Conversations

Most teachers begin to "get their feet wet" in the world of instructional conversations by asking children to solve simple word problems. IC requires teachers to pay close attention to the difficulty of the problem they are asking their students to solve. The difficulty of a problem depends on the following:

I. Can the problem be acted out?

1. Yes: Maria had 8 cookies. She gave 3 to Jose. How many cookies does Maria have now?
2. No: Maria gave 3 cookies to Jose. She started with 8 cookies. How many cookies does Maria have now?

II. Can the problem be modeled in the order it is heard?

1. Yes: Deseree had 5 cookies. Ashley gave her 8 more. How many cookies does Deseree have now?
2. No: Deseree had some cookies. Ashley gave her 8 more. Then she had 13 cookies. How many cookies did Deseree have before Ashley gave her any?

III. Can the problem be modeled directly?

1. Yes: Juan has 8 cookies. Pedro has 5 cookies. How many more cookies does Juan have?
2. No: Pedro has 5 cookies. He has 3 fewer cookies than Juan. How many cookies does Juan have?

IV. Is the unknown quantity located at the beginning, middle, or end of the problem?

1. End (easiest): Jorge had 7 cookies. He gave 4 to Julissa. How many cookies does Jorge have now?
2. Middle: Jorge had 8 cookies. He gave some to Julissa. Now he has 5 cookies. How many cookies did Jorge give to Julissa?
3. Beginning (hardest): Jorge had some cookies. He gave 3 cookies to Julissa. Then he had 5 cookies left. How many cookies did Jorge have before sharing with Julissa?

V. Can simple multiplication or division problems be acted out or modeled?

1. Multiplication: Tanya has 4 piles of cookies. There are 3 cookies in each pile. How many cookies does Tanya have?
2. Partative Division: If Kelsey gives 12 cookies to 3 friends and each friend is given the same number, how many cookies will each friend get?

Teachers need to have different types of manipulatives available when giving students problems to solve. The main focus is on the child choosing to construct his/her learning. This allows the teacher to freely walk around to check student progress. The teacher needs to make frequent stops to ask specific students how they solved the problem. Questioning should include probes in order to truly see which processes students are using to form their answer. When the majority of the students have solved their problems, the teacher then calls on a few to share their strategies with the class. As students share, the teacher can graph or chart the various strategies and post them in the room as a resource for the next time instructional conversations are used.

When students utilize the opportunity to choose a strategy and can successfully explain their thinking, they are showing their mastery at understanding the mathematical process and not just providing an answer. Once the teacher is comfortable with the knowledge of the students' stages of mathematical development, he or she can choose and/or create specific problems that target the classes' needs. This is how one can differentiate instructional conversations. Designing math time using this model will allow students to construct their knowledge and understanding for math at their own pace instead of following a textbook or the majority of the class. A teacher will not be an overnight success at the practice of instructional conversations. It takes purposeful practice, thinking, and planning, but as with anything, over time it will become second nature to the teacher and the students.

Literature Logs

Teachers can assign entries in the literature log from different segments of assigned reading. Ask the ELL student to write about personal experiences that are similar to the character and/or an event that exists in the text. After sharing personal experiences that relate to the personal experiences of the character, the teacher can then lead a discussion inviting students to share.

In the preparation of a literature unit, the teacher needs to create specific log prompts to develop what is read but also allow prompts to emerge naturally from small group discussions.

In implementing instructional conversation lessons, discussions with ELLs in small groups need to be initiated by the teacher. Participation in discussion needs to be conducted approximately forty-five minutes a week to be beneficial. These discussions not only provide an opportunity for teachers to assess comprehension, but also broaden ELLs' knowledge and understanding of the story content and themes. ELLs should not only write in their log responses to prompts or questions, but also can share in small groups or with a partner.

Literature Log Starters

1. I began to think . . .

2. I love the way . . .

3. I felt sad when . . .

4. If I were (name of character) . . .

5. I was surprised . . .

6. It seems like . . .

7. I'm not sure why . . .

8. I predict that . . .

9. I wonder . . .

10. I noticed . . .

11. This made me think of . . .

12. I can't believe . . .

13. If I wrote this book, I would . . .

14. Rate the book 1–5 and say why.

REFLECTION AND APPLICATION

1. Does the teacher spend as much or more time questioning, cueing, and prompting students to respond than explaining?

2. Does the teacher emphasize dialogue/communication in second language learning?

3. Are all students included in instructional conversations?

4. Do ELLs receive comprehensible input through the use of visuals, gestures, manipulatives, graphic organizers, and other concrete materials?

5. Does the teacher repeat, rephrase, and/or paraphrase important concepts and directions?

SIX

Strategy 6: Technologically Enriched Instruction

Technology is just a tool. In terms of getting the kids working together and motivating them, the teacher is the most important.
—Bill Gates

WHAT: DEFINING THE STRATEGY

Due to the wide range of software and hardware tools available, today's teachers have a multitude of options with which they can address the diverse needs of their students. Technology offers an almost limitless number of ways for a teacher to address student needs, including learning activities and opportunities to demonstrate comprehension. Today's students come to the learning environment with a wealth of technology knowledge, making it a familiar method for a teacher to use while also creating a comfortable learning environment for the student.

"Increasing comprehensibility in the classroom means using whatever appropriate means necessary to ensure that students understand the material presented to them" (Northwest Regional Education Lab, 2003). It is not necessary for students to understand every word or piece of information presented to them, but an overall grasp of the material is essential. Using words that an ELL already knows and understands is not the only way to increase comprehensibility. In fact, to increase ELL student advancement, it is essential to introduce new concepts and vocabulary. Spiraling new vocabulary and advanced topics with mastered material while also providing strategies that support ELL students is the best method a teacher can use.

Technology can be a wonderful source of comprehensible input and provides students with different learning styles with additional demonstrations or concrete examples of concepts being taught in the classroom. Multimedia CDs, digital tutorials, and the Web provide a near-endless source of sound, pictures, video, animation, and multimedia that can help situate learning within a meaningful context. Interacting with fellow classmates and/or real life audiences outside of their classroom provides endless opportunities for students.

Classmates working together on technology activities such as software programs in pairs, partner revisions, and writing or creating an "electronic book report" through multimedia software such as Power-Point are some of the benefits. All of these examples provide opportunities for students to learn from one another's knowledge while practicing their verbal skills, as well as their listening and responding skills, through conversation. This also promotes interacting with people outside the classroom through chat room programs, video conferencing, and email.

The opportunity to practice English skills without worrying about what others think is an advantage of utilizing technology. As Butler-Pascoe (1997) explains, "The untiring, non-judgmental nature of the computer makes it an ideal tool to help second language learners feel sufficiently secure to make and correct their own errors without embarrassment or anxiety." Another advantage of technology is in the increase in students' motivation to learn. Although the traditional paper and pencil writing assignment has its advantages, the addition of being able to use clip art, word art, colors, and different fonts are definite interest-enhancers. This does not mean that paper and pencil should be eliminated, but teachers need to realize that technology provides tremendous advantages in the classroom. The differences between a traditional bulletin board display and an animated PowerPoint can be a determinate of that extra motivation needed to capture student interest.

"Often, ELL students encounter difficulties in mastering English due to a variety of cognitive and linguistic issues" (Bray, Brown, & Green, 2004). ELL students that are struggling linguistically have a barrier in learning the content of most classrooms, which, in turn, contributes to academic and cognitive challenges. Teachers can address these challenges through technology enriched instruction using various instructional strategies to assist ELLs in more understandable learning.

WHY: THEORETICAL FRAMEWORK

- Assessing current information is only one of the benefits of technology. Through interactive technology based learning, students can take ownership of their educational process and no longer sit passively in rows while a teacher lectures (Computerland, 2012)
- Mastering computer technology in the classroom promotes self-esteem and motivates classmates to help their peers learn how to use tools such as interactive whiteboards and other methods of smart technology. In combination with working cooperatively, students are motivated to learn, making the benefits of technology crystal clear (Computerland, 2012).
- Using technology takes the focus off the textbook and assists the teacher by providing movies and audio recordings and allowing him or her to search and print out related articles and create slide show presentations to enhance lessons. Because of the ease of use, teachers are more likely to provide educationally rich supplementary materials (Yale University, 2014).
- Through the four main language domains of reading, writing, listening, and speaking, the ESL classroom develops communication skills by implementing the use of technology (Brown, 2007).
- "The act of using technology as a supplementary aid is what promotes student learning ELLs. By actively engaging students in creativity and teaching them technological and communicational aspects, students are forced to fine-tune their literacy abilities and language production skills" (Kasper & Rose, 2002).

HOW: INSTRUCTIONAL ACTIVITIES

"Top 10 Strategies for Using Technology in ELL Instruction," taken from Roblyer and Doering (2010).

1. Images downloaded from the Internet helps illustrate language concepts: helps ELL learn English and understand concept and

offers students opportunities to set in places where target language is spoken to discuss, describe and speculate about what they see.

2. Interactive storybooks support language acquisition—students can strengthen their language skills by hearing the language read to them.

3. Interactive software and handheld devices provide language skills practice—students use these resources to get individual, private feedback as they practice their language skills.

4. Presentation aids help scaffold language use. The visual formats of presentation software and videos help students demonstrate their range of language skills in nontraditional, collaborative, and engaging ways.

5. Websites offer exercises for students to practice sub-skills—online exercises are easy to access and provide intense practice in specific language skills and vocabulary sets.

6. Virtual collaborations provide authentic practice—students who work without native speakers of the target language gain both valuable language learning opportunities and intercultural insights.

7. Virtual fieldtrips provide simulated experiences—students see people in locations they could not visit otherwise.

8. Word processing—students are able to check spelling and grammar as they practice writing in the target language.

9. Language labs support language acquisition—students get personal instruction with monitoring feedback, and authentic verbal interaction.

10. Web-based authentic content—websites designed for native speakers of the target language can offer students written and oral text on topics of interest in the target language and in student's native language.

REFLECTION AND APPLICATION

1. Are web-based picture libraries used to provide visual input of content material?

2. Are digitized books used to allow students to request pronunciations and translations?

SEVEN

Strategy 7: Creating a Sense of Classroom Community

Never doubt that a small group of thoughtful, committed citizens can change the world. Indeed, that's the only thing that ever has.
—Margaret Mead

WHAT: DEFINING THE STRATEGY

Children learn best when they are part of a community and a classroom that promotes positive social skills and academic achievement can provide an excellent source. The classroom is a place where all students feel accepted and safe to be an individual. It fosters a sense of belonging and participation in class meetings, and working collaboratively is taught and modeled to resolve conflicts peacefully.

Shared meaning within an activity in which previous social or historical experiences are used to teach new subject content is the definition of co-construction. Hispanic students especially need to be assured that they are valuable and can make important contributions to society. If these opportunities to participate in the development of classroom activities and discussion is minimized by the teacher, ELLs perceive this as a message that the teacher does not care about what they have to say or about their experiences.

It is common sense that children who feel a sense of identity within groups are the most well-adjusted and successful in school. Developmentally, group interaction skills become finely tuned for students, and their "world view" expands to add a greater understanding of relationships between themselves and others. "People skills" are one of the most important skills children need for school readiness and success. This is the foundation that supports the academics to learn ABCs and 123s. That is what you are doing in the first month of school—creating an emotionally secure "home base" for children to learn in. So don't worry if you are not teaching many specific academic skills in your first month. By focusing on establishing a safe, secure, and nurturing environment, you are teaching children how to learn and are setting the stage for the entire year.

WHY: THEORETICAL FRAMEWORK

- Any program that allows a co-construction of educational activities and knowledge in the classroom can significantly improve a classroom learning environment (O'Donnell, Tharp, & Wilson, 1993).
- Co-construction of knowledge between teacher and students helps provide a sense of classroom community, as well as ensuring that instruction is relevant to students' previous knowledge (Wells & Chang-Wells, 1992).
- Many Hispanic immigrants must come to terms simultaneously with the loss of family and friends and the loss of the cultural forms (language, food, music, and art, for example) that have given the immigrants' native world a distinct and highly personal character. It is not only people who are mourned, but culture itself (Ainslie, 1998, 287).
- A community is a place where social bonds are established and individuals can flourish (Bredekamp and Rosegrant, 1992, 81).
- The opportunity to participate as a contributing member of a community is essential for children's well-being and academic success. A classroom community enables teachers to address children's basic needs, promote their resilience to hardship conditions, teach the values of respect and responsibility, and foster their social and academic competence (Wolk, 1988).

HOW: INSTRUCTIONAL ACTIVITIES

Using Identity to Build Community (Church, 2003)

Your children need to see themselves reflected in the classroom. Invite families to send in photos of their children and family before school starts or in the first few weeks. Finding themselves "already there" will go a long way toward making children feel comfortable. Not only will children enjoy finding their photos around the room, but they will also delight in learning about their new friends and their families. Children may want to make family books in the first few weeks of school as a way of getting to know each other.

Using Familiarity to Build Community (Church, 2003)

Moving into a new class of children can be very challenging. Children need to find things that are familiar to them in the classroom. It can be something simple, such as puzzles and games they might have played with in a previous classroom. While these might be materials that seem too "easy" for them, in order to build a community, children need to build a sense of comfort—the time to be challenged comes later. And, interestingly, children who have a sense of success with a particular educational material or game are more likely to share it with others and thus build community. Don't forget to use familiar and favorite songs and books at group time. Children feel so proud when they can say, "I know that book!"

Using Warmth and Beauty to Build Community (Church, 2003)

Studies have shown that warm colors and soft spaces are welcoming to children and create a secure and nurturing "nest" from which they can grow. Lots of pillows, soft toys, fresh flowers, soft clay or dough, and items for water play create a homelike environment. These elements also foster a sense of community. A soft place to share a book with a friend, a small clay table for two, or a beautiful bouquet of flowers to examine together all can create "warm spots" for children to share with a new friend. But perhaps the warmest element of your classroom is you and your *smile*.

Using Predictability to Build Community (Church, 2003)

Predictability is another important part of building an environment of trust and safety. Establishing predictable routines helps children know what to expect and helps them feel confident and capable in the group. Keep a regular schedule of activities throughout the day. If possible, take photographs of each section of the day and place them in a row at child eye-level in a left-to-right sequence from the beginning of the day to the end. If children are wondering "What comes next?" or "When do I go home?" they can look at the sequence to see how many more activities are left for the day.

Using Family Involvement to Build Community (Church, 2003)

Each child who walks through your door "comes" with a family. The family is a key ingredient to children feeling at home in your classroom. In some programs, you may only meet the families at special meetings or occasions. In others, you will have the pleasure of seeing them every day when they drop off and pick up their children. Make a point of connecting in a variety of ways, from phone calls to letters or notes sent home. If possible, learn their email addresses for instant family communication. They will appreciate your efforts and may reward you with active participation in your program. Invite family members to visit and share their culture, work, and interests. The teacher will be expanding his or her classroom community to include the greater community of the town where the school resides.

REFLECTION AND APPLICATION

1. Do students and families believe they are treated fairly by school staff?

2. Are new immigrant students carefully paired with a "buddy" who can help them navigate their new school environment?

3. Does the teacher express a personal interest in students' outside activities?

4. Do students have many opportunities to interact with positive role models?

5. Are there cross-age and peer tutoring programs to support student success in school?

6. Are mentoring programs in place to build a sense of personal efficacy and community connection?

7. Is leadership shared among students in a collaborative learning environment?

EIGHT

Strategy 8: Provide Follow-Up and Professional Development

Practice does not make perfect. Practice only makes you better, which is a great goal in itself.
—Genero Crenshaw

It isn't what you do, but how you do it.
—John Wooden

WHAT: DEFINING THE STRATEGY

Webster (as cited in Hauser, 2002) defined *professional development* as "those experiences which, systematically over a sustained period of time, enable educators to acquire and apply knowledge, understanding, skills, and abilities to achieve personal, professional, and organizational goals, and to facilitate the learning of students" (p. 2). In public schools, effective professional development affects students' learning and increases achievement when educators engage in effective professional development focused on the skills they need in order to address students' major learning challenges.

Classroom teachers want more information related to the teaching of Hispanic students, time for training and planning, and opportunities to collaborate and learn from other teachers.

It is critical for veteran teachers to have ongoing and regular opportunities to learn from each other. Ongoing professional development keeps teachers up to date on new research on how children learn, emerging technology tools for the classroom, new curriculum resources, and more. The best professional development is ongoing, experiential, collaborative, and connected to and derived from working with students and understanding their culture.

Professional development is most effective when it occurs in the context of educators' daily work. When learning is part of the school day, all educators are engaged in growth, rather than learning being limited to those who volunteer to participate on their own. School-based professional development helps educators analyze student achievement data during the school year to immediately identify learning problems, develop solutions, and promptly apply those solutions to address students' needs. Professional development also can be useful if it takes place before classes begin or after they end.

Effective professional development enables educators to develop the knowledge and skills they need to address students' learning challenges. To be effective, professional development requires thoughtful planning followed by careful implementation with feedback to ensure it responds to educators' learning needs. Educators who participate in professional development then must put their new knowledge and skills to work. Professional development is not effective unless it causes teachers to improve their instruction or causes administrators to become better school leaders.

The effectiveness of professional development depends on how carefully educators conceive, plan, and implement it. There is no substitute for rigorous thinking and execution. Unfortunately, many educators responsible for organizing professional development have had no formal education in how to do so. The learning experiences they create for others are similar to their own experiences, many of which were neither positive nor effective. As all educators on the team become more skillful, they reduce or eliminate variations in performance and begin to take collective responsibility for the success of all students, rather than for just their own.

WHY: THEORETICAL FRAMEWORK

- Teaching schedules are already crowded and a reform that simply adds work will be rejected by teachers who perceive it as not being helpful (Mehan, 1991).

- Professional development that specifically addresses improving Hispanic student education is needed (Jimenez & Barrera, 2000).
- For professional development to be successful, it should aim to enhance and expand a teacher's tool kit of instructional strategies instead of radically altering it (Gersten & Woodward, 1992; Richardson, 1990; Smylie, 1988).
- "Synthesis of research on effective school based programs for Hispanic students have found that there are several characteristics common to successful programs:
  a. Have well specified goals
  b. Provide ample opportunity for teacher professional development
  c. Begin early and are maintained throughout school experience
  d. Include ongoing assessment and feedback
  e. Incorporate the use of tutors and other support staff
  f. Focus on quality of implementation" (Fashola et al., 2001).
- Stand-alone workshops have less than a 5 percent chance of effecting a change in teacher practice. If you add ongoing professional development allowing teachers to collaborate with their colleagues and supplement with ongoing support from coaches and administrative staff, the effect on the teaching and learning increases to 90 percent (Joyce and Showers, 2002; Lockwood, 2001).
- The models of teaching and learning with which many teachers are familiar have a primary emphasis on rote memorization and little emphasis on a deeper understanding of a subject (Cohen, McLaughlin, & Talbert, 1993; Darling-Hammond & McLaughlin, 1995; Porter & Brophy, 1988). Utilizing a more balanced approach that has the primary focus on understanding subject matter allows teachers to learn more about the subjects they teach. This continual deepening of knowledge and skills is an important part of the teaching profession (National Board for Professional Teaching Standards, 1989; Shulman & Sparks, 1992).

HOW: INSTRUCTIONAL ACTIVITIES

Success for All (SFA)

SFA is an intervention that begins early in at-risk students' academic lives; tutoring is done in twenty-minute blocks and is facilitated by certified teachers. Evaluations of SFA have indicated that the program has demonstrated consistent positive results for Hispanic students when implemented with fidelity (Lockwood, 2001; Slavin & Madden, 2001).

Reading Recovery/Descubriendo La Lectura

This early intervention program focuses on the lowest-achieving readers in the first grade (Pinnell, 1989). Students receive one-on-one tutoring for thirty minutes a day for twelve to twenty weeks. Tutors are certified teachers who have had one year of training in reading recovery. Getting to know the student and their difficulties is key; the program then builds into more structured activities, including reading familiar stories, writing a message, or reading a new book (Escamilla, 1994).

Consistency Management and Cooperative Discipline/Disciplina Consistete y Cooperativa *(CMCD)*

CMCD is a school-wide program emphasizing students' and staffs' shared responsibility for making and keeping rules that maintain safety and order, largely through emphasizing caring, prevention, cooperation, organization, and a sense of community. Students and staff, including support staff such as office aides and custodians, enforce the rules. Evaluations document dramatic reductions in rates of serious and minor behavior (Freiberg, Stein, & Huang, 1995) and teachers report having up to forty minutes more each day to use on academics (Opuni, 2005).

REFLECTION AND APPLICATION

1. Does follow-up professional development ensure provisions for immediate implementation into the classroom?

2. Are support mechanisms in place to ensure accountability for follow-up support?

3. Do teachers receive coaching (a provision by which a colleague or an "expert" is available) to support teachers' efforts to apply new practices to their classroom?

4. Is acceptable time allotted so that (while supervised) the teacher can achieve mastery of the skill? Miles & Huberman (1994) claim it may take six to eighteen months for mastery, while Joyce & Showers (1980) found that ten to fifteen practices, with feedback, of a specific skill or teaching strategy are needed.

NINE

Strategy 9: Complex Instruction

More often than not, family members are interacting with you based on old and often inaccurate perceptions, not current reality. Take that into account.
—Alan Weiss

WHAT: DEFINING THE STRATEGY

Elizabeth Cohen and her colleagues at Stanford University are credited with developing a form of cooperative learning known as Complex Instruction (CI). Complex instruction is a research-based, cooperative learning approach designed for academically and linguistically diverse classrooms. Group work is carefully crafted with the goal of providing all students access to engaging, higher order learning activities. The group work resembles cooperative learning in that it utilizes norms and group roles. CI differs, however, in the assumptions made as to why (or why not) students participate in collaborative learning groups. Students at different levels of academic achievement can successfully work together in completing group projects due to the use of multiple ability curricula (Oakes, 2005).

WHY: THEORETICAL FRAMEWORK

- "CI's approach to group work is ideal for classrooms serving Hispanic students as it offers culturally relevant, intellectually challenging curriculum" (Oakes, 2005).

- It is well known that through the use of CI's multiple ability tasks, students talk and work together more often (Oakes, 2005).
- Because students practice the skills in CI for real purposes like communication, contribution, and understanding, it improves language skills and improves low-achieving, disengaged readers' reading and writing skills (Oakes, 2005).
- The skills of talking and working together are the key to successful group learning (Cohen, Lotan, and Holthius, 1995).

HOW: INSTRUCTIONAL ACTIVITIES

Using a range of instructional and management strategies, teachers can differentiate through complex instruction. These strategies include the implementation of role training, group accountability, and group-worthy tasks.

According to Tomlinson (1995), there are three main categories to base decisions on how to group students: readiness, interest, and learning profile.

Readiness

Vygotsky (1978, 1986) uses the term "zone of proximal development" (ZPD) referring to a point of required mastery where a child cannot successfully function alone, but can succeed with scaffolding or support. "Instruction should always 'be in advance' of a child's current level of mastery. That is, teachers should teach within a child's zone of proximal development. If material is presented at or below the mastery level, there will be no growth. If presented well above the zone, children will be confused and frustrated" (Byrnes, 1996, p. 33).

The types of strategies used at this level are:

Multiple Intelligence
"Jigsaw" Activities
Taped Material
Anchor Activities
Varying Organizers
Varied Texts
Varied Supplemental Materials
Literature Circles

Interest

Interest-based study is linked to motivation and appears to promote positive impacts on learning in both the short and long term (Herbert, 1993; Renninger, 1990, 1998; Tobias, 1994). To enhance motivation, productivity, and achievement, teachers need to draw on student interests to modify instruction (Amabile, 1996; Torrance, 1995). Students that are interested in the questions and tasks presented are much more likely to become more engaged and have a sense that the work they are doing is rewarding. This also leads to increased creativity and productivity, as well as a higher degree of student autonomy and intrinsic motivation (Amabile, 1983; Brunner, 1961; Collins & Amabile, 1999; Sharan & Sharan, 1992).

Interest-based strategies include:

Tiered Lessons
Tiered Centers
Tiered Products
Learning Contracts
Small Group Instruction
Group Investigation Orbitals
Independent Study

Learning Profile

"As it is beneficial to student learning for teachers to respond to their readiness levels and interests, it also appears beneficial to address student variance in learning profile. Learning profile attends to efficiency of learning" (Tomlinson, 2003). A student's preferred mode of learning is referred to their learning profile and can be affected by a number of factors including learning style, intelligence preference, gender, and culture.

"Learning styles theory points to individual preferences related to categories, such as environment, emotions, interactions, and physical needs, suggesting that such factors as light, temperature, seating arrangements, demand for concentration, degree of learner mobility, time of day, and perceptual mode impact learning" (e.g., Dunn, 1996). A meta-analysis of research on learning styles (Sullivan, 1993) reported that the use of flexible teaching or counseling when addressing a student's learning style will most likely result in improved achievement and attitude goals.

Learning profile strategies include:

- 4-MAT
- Varied questioning
- Strategies
- Interest centers
- Interest groups
- Varied homework
- Compacting
- Varied journal prompts
- Complex instruction

Ways to Differentiate Content

- Books on tape
- Highlights on tape
- Reading partners/Reading buddies

> Read/summarize
> Read/question/answer
> Visual organizer/summarize
> Parallel reading with teacher prompt

- Choral reading/Antiphonal reading
- Flipbooks
- New American lecture
- Split Journals (double-entry/triple-entry)
- Digests/"Cliff Notes"
- Note taking organizers
- Varied texts
- Varied supplementary materials

Here's how it works: Using a group-worthy task, the teacher needs to make sure students are ready. To do this, students must understand the roles they are expected to play, be given clear and detailed instructions about how they should work together and once the task is completed, what the student should do.

A group-worthy task is one that:

- is open-ended
- is based on discovery
- requires multiple abilities

- is challenging
- can be represented in more than one way

Roles for Group Members

Before groups get started, the teacher needs to provide plenty of coaching on what the roles and responsibilities are, how to work productively, and what the task is. Once the group understands the roles, the majority of the energy will be spent on working productively and not on how to do the task. Suggested group roles are:

- *The Facilitator* asks if everyone understands what's been said and if anyone has a question.
- *The Team Captain* keeps the group on task, reminds people of how they're supposed to proceed, and makes sure everyone's ideas are heard.
- *The Resource Manager* makes sure all conversations happen in the middle of the table, collects materials from the teacher, calls the teacher over when the whole group has a question, and returns materials.
- *The Recorder* takes notes on the ideas, questions, and hypotheses, prepares the group's presentation paper, and makes sure everyone can explain the group's solution.

Bolster students of low status by identifying multiple abilities

There are many conditions that can label a student as low status, including language accent, ethnic appearance, lower socioeconomic background, and perceived reading and academic ability. These children have experienced rejection of their ideas or exclusion from projects. As the student withdraws from the group, their intellectual development is stifled. To address this, the teacher needs to emphasize that the group has multiple abilities and every member has something to contribute to the project. This expectation requires all students to be brought into the interaction and results in students seeking contributions from each other creating healthy peer pressure.

Raise the expectations for competence

Negative perceptions can be reversed by having the teacher acknowledge the capabilities of low status students to the group. The trust students have in their teacher and their opinions increases the chance that students will acknowledge previously ignored peers.

Develop student responsibility for each other's performance and learning

When the group roles are interdependent, each student will have some responsibility in the success of others. In order to maintain this climate, create roles such as facilitator, harmonizer, and reporter, which will help members assume responsibility for the performance of others.

Promote higher order thinking

Selecting appropriate tasks for student groups promotes higher order thinking and is the main purpose of CI. Topics and tasks that are open-ended require multiple-input points of view and high level interactions need to be chosen by the teacher.

REFLECTION AND APPLICATION

1. Are there established collaborative norms in the classroom?

2. Have you taken the time to teach children how to take on group processing roles in their small groups?

3. Do you delegate authority for learning to the learners in the classroom?

4. What are you doing to modify or create rich group tasks?

TEN

Strategy 10: Defining and Understanding Citizenship

. . . ordinary men and women may often feel unmotivated to exert their citizenship, either because they cannot tell the difference between the different alternatives, or because they have lost faith in the political classes, or because they feel that the really important issues are not in their power to decide.
—Patricio Aylwin Azócar

WHAT: DEFINING THE STRATEGY

Like most immigrants, Hispanics are chasing the American dream: democratic government open and responsive to the people. "Public schools, however, no longer teach them how to become Americans. Latino students' extraordinary high dropout rate is related, in part, to their lack of attachment to a school and a sense of not fitting in to the campus or classroom culture" (Grandara, 2010). Schools need to implement successful assimilation models, but these models do not have to be unique to immigrant students. Emphasizing civic responsibility and good citizenship needs to be a focus in today's schools. Examples of such events include Election Day Mock Voting, Veterans Day Memorial Program, and 9/11 Remembrance (Rangel, 2013).

Many Hispanic students' understanding of norms, standards, and expectations of US society are inhibited due to lack of access to peers from mainstream US culture. Many of these students may rarely come in contact with anyone who has gone to college or who intends to go, so aspirations of going to college never develop.

Cultural elements are valued as we grow. Just as the music we like, the clothes we wear, and the cars we drive, we are not born knowing what we like. "Through enculturation, the process of communicating a group's culture from generation to generation, you learned what you liked by choosing from among the elements available within your culture" (Smith, 1966). Information is communicated about the elements of your choices through colleagues, the media, and — most importantly — your family. Cultures are constantly changing as new information and influences cross our path. Scientific discoveries are one source of change, but others take place through acculturation, "where we acquire other approaches, beliefs, and values by coming into contact with other cultures" (Smith, 1966).

WHY: THEORETICAL FRAMEWORK

- Obtaining civil and legal rights is a primary reason that one in five (18 percent) of naturalized Hispanics gave to pursue US citizenship (Taylor et al., 2012).
- Of the Hispanics that cite family reasons for becoming a US citizen, half state their naturalization was a parental decision. The respondents were brought to the US as children and chose to become naturalized or were naturalized as minors when their parents became citizens.
- Another important reason Hispanics state for becoming naturalized is having members of the family who are US citizens. The main motivation for foreign-born Hispanic US citizens is to become a sponsor for a family member to migrate legally to the United States.
- A small share of naturalized Hispanics state that they obtained their citizenship for family or for their children.

HOW: INSTRUCTIONAL ACTIVITIES

1. Collaborate with students as to what citizenship means. This discussion should include rights and responsibilities of citizens.
2. Allow students to share personal stories and define their view of what makes a good citizen. For example:

- I helped a new child from a different country.
- I volunteered to pick up trash at the park.
- My mom and I walked around the neighborhood passing out pamphlets to vote.
- I helped needy children by collecting and donating used toys and clothes.
- When a student threatened to fight me, I walked away.
- When approached by another student to help them steal, I said "No."
- I follow all the bicycle safety rules and wear my helmet.
- To cross the street, I use the crosswalk and wait for the signal.

3. Have students imagine what the world would be like if there were no rules or laws at school, at home, in traffic, or other places.
4. Always involve students in making or changing classroom rules, as well as deciding the consequences. Students are more likely to "buy in" and follow rules they are involved in making.
5. Invite veterans, immigrants, or people who lived through the Great Depression to speak to students. Collaborate to come up with questions students can ask these visitors, such as:

- How do you feel about the United States of America?
- Tell me about your life.
- What was a difficult time for you?
- What does being a US citizen mean to you?

Have the children write about or draw what they discovered, report their findings and post the results on a bulletin board.
6. Write poems, stories, songs, and plays about citizenship and have students perform them to help make connections and have a deeper understanding of what citizenship means.
7. Have students design thank you cards for local citizens that generously contribute to the good of the community.
8. Find newspaper or magazine articles on various topics concerning civic life and have students read, analyze, and debate them.

9. Create a video on "American Life," which can be a unique way to assist ELLs in understanding citizenship.

10. Invite knowledgeable speakers of United States history or specific historical characters to bring detailed information into the classroom.

11. Make available for the students stories about extraordinary Americans that they can read. Finding Hispanic American stories is even more beneficial.

12. Present detailed lesson units on the Declaration of Independence, the United States Constitution, and the Bill of Rights to deepen students' understanding.

13. Have students take photos of their community and create a classroom book entitled "Our Freedoms," "Our Citizens," or "Being an American."

14. As a class, attend city council meetings, school board meetings, or court sessions, or museums, monuments, and national parks, all of which are great opportunities to learn.

15. Research American symbols and songs like the "Star Spangled Banner" and/or the Pledge of Allegiance for their significance.

16. Buddy students with younger students and have them create a presentation about the American flag history or symbolism.

17. Engage in deep discussions about taxes, income, and public professions like police, fireman, prison guards, and postal workers.

18. Implement a student council model and have students run for representatives and vote.

19. Participate in community service projects like recycling, picking up litter, and volunteering to encourage good citizenship.

REFLECTION AND APPLICATION

1. Is there mutual respect and collaboration among administrators, teachers, students, parents, and the community? If not, what is the barrier?

2. Does mutual trust and positive interactions among diverse students, faculty, and administration exist? If not, what are the barriers?

3. What is the purpose of and approaches to pupil assessment in citizenship education?

4. Does classroom instruction explicitly focus on meaningful civic content?

5. What are the ongoing issues, challenges, and possibilities in the development of effective practices in citizenship education?

6. Is student input sought for planning and skills in participatory problem solving?

7. Are effective practices and strategies in place for assessing pupils' learning and achievement in citizenship education?

8. Is there a welcoming and participating environment for students?

9. Is the school climate supportive of civic involvement?

Glossary of Key Terms

At-Risk: A student who, because of his or her circumstances, is statistically more likely than others to fail academically.

CRT (Culturally Responsive Teaching): Using a student's cultural knowledge, prior experiences, and performance style to make learning more appropriate.

ELL (English Language Learner): A person who is learning the English language in addition to his or her native language.

ESL (English as a Second Language): The use or study of English by speakers with a different native language.

Hispanic: Broadly refers to the culture, peoples, or nations with a historical link to Spain. For the purpose of this book, "Hispanic" is used to define a student population born in Mexico or Central America, which is where the majority of the Hispanic students derive here in the Southwestern U.S.

Immigrant: People who move to and settle in a country to which they are not native. For the purpose of this book, "immigrants" refers to Hispanics moving to the United States from Mexico.

Poverty: The state of being in which one lacks a certain amount of material possession or money and lacks basic capacity to participate effectively in society.

References

Ainslie, R. C. (1998). Cultural mourning, immigration and engagement: Vignettes from the Mexican experience. In M. M. Suarez-Orozco, *Mexican immigration in interdisciplinary perspectives* (285–305). Cambridge, MA: Harvard University Press.

Alexander, D., Heaviside, S. & Farris, E. (1999). Status of education reform in public Elementary and secondary schools: Teacher's perspectives. Washington, DC: U.S. Department of Education, National Center for Education Statistics.

Alliance for Excellent Education (AEE). (2011). The high cost of high school dropouts: What the nation pays for inadequate high schools. Issue brief. Retrieved from www.all4ed.org/files/highcost.pdf.

Alliance for Excellent Education. (2006). Healthier and wealthier: Decreasing health care costs by increasing educational attainment. Retrieved from www.all4ed.org/files/handW.pdf.

American Psychological Association. (2012). Facing the school dropout dilemma. Retrieved from www.apa.org/pi/families/resources/school-dropout-prevention.

Applebee, A. N. & Langer, J. A. (1983). Instructional scaffolding: Reading and writing as natural language activities. *Language Arts* 60: 168–175.

Astin, A. W. (1982). *Minorities in American higher education*. San Francisco, CA: Jossey-Bass.

August, D. & Shanahan, L. (2006). Developing literacy in second language learners: Report of the national literacy panel on language minority children and youth. Washington, DC: National Literacy Panel on Language, Minority Children and Youth.

Beebe, S. A., Beebe, S. J., & Redmond, U. V. (2005). *Interpersonal communication: Relating to others* (4th ed.). Boston, MA: Pearson.

Bernardo, A. I. (2005). Language and modeling word problems in mathematics among bilinguals. *The Journal of Psychology*, 139(5): 413–425.

Borman, G. & Dowling, N. M. (2012). Schools and inequality: A multilevel analysis of Coleman's Inequality of Educational Opportunity Data.

Bray, M., Brown, A., & Green, T. D. (2004). *Technology and the diverse learner: A guide to classroom practice*. Thousand Oaks, CA: Corwin Press.

Bredekamp, S. & Rosegrant, T. (1992). *Reaching potentials: Appropriate curriculum and assessment for young children*. Washington, DC: National Association for the Education of Young Children.

Brown, H. D. (2007). *Teaching by principles: An interactive approach to language pedagogy. Technology in the Classroom*. White Plains, NY: Pearson Education.

Buschman, L. (2011). Using student interviews to guide classroom instruction: An action research project. *Teaching Children Mathematics* 8: 222–227.

Butler-Pascoe, M. E. (1997). Technology and second language learners: The promise and the challenge ahead. *American Language Review* 1: 20–22.

Calderon, M. (1991). Benefits of cooperative learning for Hispanic students. *Texas Research Journal* 2: 39–57.

Campbell, J. R., Hombo, C. M., & Mazzeo, J. (2000). NAEP 1999: Trends in academic Progress (NCES Report No 2000-469). Washington, DC: U.S. Department of Education.

Cazden, C. (2001). The language of learning and teaching, second edition. Portsmouth, NH: Heinemann.

Center for American Progress. (2012). America's leaky pipeline for teachers of color. Retrieved from www.cdn.american progress.org.

Chen, Z. & Kaplan, H. (2003). School failure in early adolescence and status attainment in middle adulthood: A longitudinal study. *Sociology of Education* 76(2): 110–127.

Cheung, A. & Slavin, R. (2005). Effective reading programs for English Language Learners and other language minority students. *Bilingual Research Journal* 29, 241–267.

Christian, D. (1995). Two-way bilingual education. In C. L. Montone (Ed.), *Teaching linguistically and culturally diverse learners. Effective programs and practices,* 8–11. Santa Cruz, CA: National Center for Research on Cultural Diversity and Second Language Learning.

Church, E. (2003). Building community in the classroom. Retrieved from http://stage30.scholastic.com/browse/article.jsp?d=3749832.

Center for Mental Health in Schools, UCLA. (2007). Dropout prevention. The School of Mental Health Project, Department of Psychology. Los Angeles, CA: Author.

Clark, N. (2013). An overview of education in Mexico. World Educations News & Reviews. Retrieved from http://wenr.wes.org/2013/05/wenr-may-2013-an-overview-of-education-in-mexico.

Cochran-Smith, M. (2004). *Walking the road: Race, diversity and social justice in teacher education.* New York: Teachers College Press.

Cohen, A. D. (1998). *Strategies in learning and using a second language.* Harlow, Essex: Longman.

Cohen, D. K., McLaughlin, M. W. & Talbert, J. E. (1993). *Teaching for understanding Challenges for policy and practice.* San Francisco, CA: Jossey-Bass.

Cohen, E. G., Lotan, R. A., & Holthuis, N. (1995). Talking and working together: Conditions for learning in complex instruction. In M. T. Hallinan (Ed.), *Restructuring Schools: Promising Practices and Policies,* 157–174. New York: Plenum Press.

Computerland. (2012). Benefits of technology in the classroom. Retrieved from http://www.computerlandtexas.com/benefits-of-technology-classroom.php.

Costantini, C. (2012). What the Latino achievement gap really looks like. Retrieved from http://fusion.net/american_dream/story.

Darling-Hammond, L. & McLaughlin, M. W. (1995). Policies that support professional development in an era of reform. *Phi Delta Kappan* 76(8): 597–604.

Davis, C. P. (2001). The evolution of pedagogical changes in a multicultural context. Unpublished doctoral dissertation, University of Virginia, Charlottesville.

DeRuy, E. (2012). 8th grade Latino students behind their white, Asian peers. Retrieved from http://www.fusion-net/american-dream/story/us-hispanic-students.

Dynarski, M. & Gleason, P. (2002). How can we help? What we have learned from recent federal dropout prevention evaluations. *Journal for Education of Students Placed at Risk* 7, 43–69.

Ellis, R. (2005). Principles of instructed language learning. *System* 33: 209–224.

Escamilla, K. (1994). Descubriendo la lectura: An early intervention literacy program In Spanish literacy. *Teaching and Learning* 1, 57–70.

Fashola, O. S., Slavin, R. E., Calderon, M., & Duran, R. (2001). Effective programs for Latino students in elementary and middle schools. In R.E. Slavin and M. Calderon (Eds.), *Effective programs for Latino students*, 1–66. Mahwah, NJ: Lawrence Erlbaum.

Fillmore, L. W. & Snow, C. E. (2000). What teachers need to know about language. Washington, DC: Center for Applied Linguistics.

Frankenberg, E. & Siegel-Hawley, G. (2008). Are teachers prepared for racially changing schools? University of California Civil Rights Project. Retrieved from http://civilrightsproject.ucla.edu/research/k-12-education/integration-and-diversity/are-teachers-prepared-for-racially-changing-schools/frankenberg-are-teachers-prepared-racially.pdf

Freeman, D. E. & Freeman, Y. S. (2001). *Between worlds: Access to second language acquisition* (2nd Ed.). Portsmouth, NH: Heinemann.

Freiberg, H. J., Stein, T., & Huang, S. (1995). The effects of classroom management Intervention on student achievement in inner-city elementary schools. *Educational Research and Evaluation* 1(1): 33–66.

Fry, R. (2003). Hispanic youth dropping out of U.S. schools: Measuring the challenge. PEW Hispanic Report. Retrieved from http://pewhispanic.org/files/reports/ 19.pdf.

Fuller, B. & Coll, C. G. (2010). Learning from Latinos: Contexts, families, and child Development in motion: Introduction to the specials section. *Developmental Psychology* 46(3), 559–565.

Gandara, J., Maxwell-Jolly, J., & Driscoll, A. (2005). *Listening to teachers of English learners*. Santa Cruz, CA: Center for the Future of Teaching and Learning. Retrieved from http://www.cftl.org/documents/2005/listeningforweb.pdf.

Gandora, P. (2010). Special topic/The Latino education crisis. *Educational Leadership*, 67(6), 24–30.

Garcia, E. (1999). *Student cultural diversity: Understanding and meeting the challenge* (2nd ed.). New York: Houghton Mifflin.

Garcia, E. (1994). *Understanding and meeting the challenge of students' cultural diversity*. Boston, MA: Houghton Mifflin.

Gay, G. (2000). *Culturally responsive teaching: Theory, research & practice*. New York: Teachers College Press.

Gersten, R. & Woodward, J. (1992). The quest to translate research into classroom practice: Strategies for assisting classroom teachers work with at-risk students and students with disabilities. In D. Carnine & E. Kamcenui (Eds.), *Higher Cognitive Functioning for All Students*, 201–218, Austin, TX: Pro-Ed.

Goldenberg, C. (1991). Learning to read in New Zealand: The balance of skills and meaning. *Language Arts* 68, 555–562.

Goldenberg, C., & Patthey-Chavez, G. (1995). Discourse processes in instructional Conversations: interactions between teacher and transition students. *Discourse Processes* 19:1, p. 57–73.

Gollnick, D. M. & Chinn, P. C. (2009). *Multicultural education in a pluralistic society*. Upper Saddle River, NJ: Pearson Prentice Hall.

Gonzalez, N., Moll, L., Floyd-Tenery, M., Rivera, A., Rendon, P., Gonzalez, R., & Amanti, C. (1993). Teacher research on funds of knowledge: Learning from households. Report of the National Center for Research on Cultural Diversity and Second Language Learning. Tucson: University of Arizona.

Grandara, P. (2010). The Latino education crisis. *Educational Leadership*, 64, p. 24–30.

Gudykunst, W. B. (1998). *Bridging differences: Effective intergroup communication.* Newbury Park, CA: Sage.

Haberman, M. (1991). Pedagogy of poverty versus good teaching. *Phi Delta Kappan* 73: 290–294.

Hadre, P. L. & Reeve, J. (2003). A motivational model of rural students' intentions to persist in, versus drop out of, high school. *Journal of Educational Psychology* 95: 347–356.

Hamayan, E. V. (1990). Preparing mainstream classroom teachers to teach potentially English proficient students. Washington, DC, U.S. Department of Education. Office of Bilingual Education and Minority Languages.

Hammond, C., Linton, D., Smink, J., & Drew. S. (2007). Dropout risk factors and exemplary programs: A technical report. Clemson, SC: National Dropout Prevention Center/Network.

Hanushek, A. E. & Jorgenson, W. W. (1996). Improving America's schools: The role of incentives. Board on Science, Technology and Economic Policy. National Research Council.

Hauser, B. (2002). *Question and answer handbook for professional development.* Frankfort, KY: Department of Education.

Haveman, R. H. & Wolfe, B. (1983). Have disability transfers caused the decline in older male labor force participation? Institute for Research on Poverty discussion paper. University of Wisconsin.

Hoosain, E. (2000). The need for interviews in the mathematics classroom. Humanistic *Mathematic Network Journal* 22: 16–18.

Iowa Department of Education. (2013). Education statistics on English Language Learners. Retrieved from www.educationiowa.gov/education-statistics.

Irvine, J. J. (2003). *Educating teachers for diversity: Seeing with a cultural eye.* New York: Teachers College Press.

Jensen, E. (2013). Engaging students with poverty in mind: Practical strategies for raising achievement. Alexandria, VA: Association for Supervision and Curriculum Development.

Jimenez, R. T. & Barrera, R. (2000). How will bilingual/ESL programs in literacy change in the next millennium? *Reading Research Quarterly* 35: 522–523.

Joyce, B. & Showers, B. (2002). *Student achievement through staff development* (3rd ed.). Alexandria, VA: Association for Supervision and Curriculum Development.

Kagan, S. (1994). *Cooperative learning.* San Clemente, CA: Kagan Cooperative.

Kasper, G. & Rose, K. R. (2002). *Pragmatic development in a second language.* Oxford: Blackwell.

Kasper, L. F. (2010). New technologies, new literacies focus discipline research and ESL learning communities. *Language Learning and Technology* 4(2). Retrieved from http://llt.msu.edu/vol4num2/Kasper/default.html.

Kindler, A. (2002). Survey of the states' limited English proficiency students and available educational programs and services 2000–2001 (summary report). Washington, DC: National Clearinghouse for English Language Acquisition and Language Instruction Educational Programs.

Knapp, M. S. et al. (1995). *Teaching for meaning in high poverty classrooms.* New York: Teachers College Press.

Laird, J., Kienzl, G., DeBell, M., & Chapman, C. (2007). Dropout rates in the United States: 2005. (NCES 2007-059). U.S. Department of Education, National Center for Educational Statistics.

Langer, J. (2002). *Effective literacy instruction: Building successful reading and writing programs*. Urbana, IL: National Council of Teachers of English.

Lare, J., Lew, L., & Chapman, C. D. (2006). Dropout rates in the United States: 2002, 2003 (NCES 2006-062). U.S. Department of Education, National Center for Educational Statistics. Retrieved from http://nces.ed.gov/pubs2006/2006062.pdf.

Lesaux, N. & Rangel, J. (2013). How can schools best educate Hispanic students? Latinos Ready to Vote, latinosreadytovote.com.

Lochner, L., & Moretti, E. (2004). The effect of education on crime: Evidence from prison inmates, arrests and self reports. *American Economic Review* 94(1), 155–189.

Lockwood, A.T. (2001). Effective elementary, middle and high school programs for Latino Youth. In R. E. Slavin and M. Calderon (Eds.), *Effective Programs for Latino Students*, 101–24. Mahwah, NJ: Lawrence Erlbaum.

Loeb, S., Fuller, B., Kagan, S. L., & Carrol, B. (2004). Childcare in poor communities: Early learning effects on type, quality, and stability. *Child Development* 75: 47–65.

McGee, K. (2012). How cultural differences may affect student performance. Retrieved from www.greatschools.org/special-education/support/704-cultural differences-student-perfomance.

Mehan, H. (1991). Sociological foundations supporting the study of cultural diversity (Research Report No. 1). Santa Cruz, CA, and Washington, DC: National Center for Research on Cultural Diversity and Second Language Learning.

Melendez, M. (1993). Bilingual education in California: A status report. *Thrust for Educational Leadership* 22, 35–38.

Menken, K. & Holmes, P. (2000). Ensuring English language learners' success: Balancing teacher quantity with quality. Washington, DC: NCBE.

MetLife. (2001). The MetLife survey of the American teacher 2001. Key elements of quality schools. Retrieved from www.ced.org/docs/report/report survey_american_teacher01.pdf.

Migration Policy Institute. (2011). Mexican and Central American immigrants in the U.S. Retrieved from www.migrationpolicy.org.

Miles, M. B. & Huberman, A. M. (1994). Qualitative data analysis. Thousand Oaks, CA: Sage.

Miller, L. S. (1995). *An American imperative: Accelerating minority educational advancement*. Binghamton, NY: Vail-Ballou Press.

Moh, K., Mohr, A. J., & Mohr, E. (2007). Extending English Language Learners classroom interactions: Using the response protocol. Reading Rockets. Retrieved from www.readingrockets.org.

Moll, L., Amanti, C., Neff, D. & Gonzalez, N. (1992). Funds of knowledge for teaching: Using a qualitative approach to connect homes and classrooms. *Theory into Practice* 31(2): 132–140.

National Board for Professional Teaching Standards. (1989). Toward high and rigorous standards for the teaching profession. Washington, DC.

National Center for Educational Statistics. (NCES). (2011). Characteristics of at-risk students in NELS:88. U.S. Department of Education Office of Educational Research and Improvement.

National Council of Supervisors of Mathematics. (NCSM). (1977). Position paper on basic mathematical skills. Golden, CO: Author.

National Council of Teachers of Mathematics. (NCTM). (1980). An agenda for action: Recommendations for school mathematics for the 1980s. Reston, VA: Author.

NCTM. (1989). Curriculum and evaluation standards for school mathematics. Reston, VA: Author.

NCTM. (2000). Principles and standards for school mathematics. Reston, VA: Author.

National Research Council. (2006). *Hispanics and the future of America.* Washington, DC: National Academies Press.

Noor, R. (2012). Four approaches to incorporating cultural diversity into classroom Curriculum. Retrieved from http://voices.yahoo.com/four-approaches-incorporating-cultural-diversity-10840943.html.

Northwest Regional Education Lab. (2003). ELD, English language development. Retrieved from http://schoolsweb.dysart.org/Edtech/content.aspx?

Oakes, J. (2005). *Keeping track: How schools structure inequality* (2nd ed.). New Haven, CT: Yale University Press.

O'Donnell, C. R., Tharp, R. G., & Wilson, K. (1993). Activity settings as the unit of analysis: A theoretical basis for community intervention and development. *American Journal of Community Psychology* 21: 501–520.

Ogbu, J. U. (1995). Understanding cultural diversity and learning. In the *Handbook of Research on Multicultural Education.* New York: Macmillan.

Olneck, M. R. (1995). Immigrants and education. In *Handbook of research on Multicultural Education.* Edited by J. A. Banks and C.A.M. Banks. New York: Macmillan.

Opuni, K.A. (2005). Project GRAD Newark: Program evaluation report (2003–04). Center for Research on School Reform (CRSR). University of St. Thomas, Houston, TX.

Orrenius, P. & Zavodny, M. (2011). Trends in poverty and inequality among Hispanics. Working papers 1109, Federal Reserve Bank of Dallas.

Ortiz, A. A. (1997). Learning disabilities occurring concomitantly with linguistic Differences. *Journal for Learning Disabilities* 30: 321–332.

Ortiz, A. A. & Wilkinson, C. Y. (1991). Assessment and intervention model for the bilingual Exceptional student. *Teacher Education and Special Education* 14: 35–42.

Ortiz, S. O. (2001). Assessment of cognitive abilities in Hispanic children. *Seminars In Speech and Language* 22(1): 17–37.

Padron, Y. N. & Knight, S. L. (1989). Linguistic and cultural influences on classroom Instruction. In H. P. Baptiste, J. Anderson, J. Walker de Felix & H. C. Waxman (Eds.), *Leadership, equity and school effectiveness*, 173–185. Newbury Park, CA: Sage.

Padron, Y. N. & Waxman, H. C. (1993). Teaching and learning risks associated with limited cognitive mastery in science and mathematics for limited English proficient students. Proceedings of the third national research symposium on limited English proficient students, 2, 511–547.

Padron, Y. N., Waxman, H. C., & Rivera, H. L. (2002). Issues in educating Hispanic students, In S. Stringfield & D. Land (Eds.), *Educating at risk students.* Chicago: National Society for the Study of Education.

Paris, S. G. & Cross, D. R. (1983). Ordinary learning: Pragmatic connections among children's beliefs, motives and actions. In J. Bisanz, G. Bisanz, & R. Kail (Eds.), *Learning in Children*, 137–169. New York: Springer-Verlag.

Paris, S. G., Lipson, M. Y., & Wixson, K. K. (1994). Becoming a strategic reader. In R. B. Ruddell & H. Singer (Eds.) *Theoretical Models and Processes of Reading*, 788–811. Newark, DE: International Reading Association.

Perez, B. (1996). Instructional conversations as opportunities for English language acquisition for culturally and linguistically diverse students. *Language Arts* 73(3): 173.

PEW Hispanic Center. (2011). Hispanic trends project. Retrieved from www.pewhispanic.org.

Pinnell, G. S. (1989). Reading recovery: Helping at-risk children learn to read. *Elementary School Journal* 90: 161–182.

Porter, A. & Brophy, J. (1988). Synthesis of research on good teaching: Insights from the work of the Institute for Research on Teaching. Educational Leadership 45 (8), 74–85. (Also Occasional Paper No. 114, East Lansing: Michigan State University, Institute for Research on Teaching, 1987; a chapter in R. S. Brandt [Ed.], Readings on research from educational leadership [217–226]. Alexandria, VA: Association for Supervision and Curriculum Development; a chapter in Readings from educational leadership: Coaching and staff development [66–75], a companion volume edited by R. S. Brandt for ASCD.)

Pressley, M. (2006). What the future of reading research could be. Paper presented at the international Reading Associations Reading Research, Chicago, IL.

Rajagopal, K. (2011). Create success. Association for Supervision and Curriculum Development, Alexandria, VA.

Rangel, R. (2013). Latinas in leadership generations taking action (rountable discussion). National Multicultural Conference and Summit, Houston, TX.

Reyes, P., Scribner, J. D., & Scribner, A.P. (1999). *Lessons from high performing Hispanic schools*. New York: Teachers College Press.

Richardson, V. (1990). Significant and worthwhile change in teacher practice. *Educational Researcher* 19: 10–18.

Riordin, J. & Noyce, P. (2001). The impact of two standards based mathematics curricula on student achievement in Massachusetts. *Journal for Research in Mathematics Education* 32(4): 368–398.

Rist, R.C. (1973). *The urban school: A factory for failure. A study of education in American society.* Cambridge: MIT Press.

Rivera, C. & Zehler, A. M. (1991). Assuring the academic success of language minority Students: Collaboration in teaching and learning. *Journal of Education* 173: 52–77.

Roblyer, M. D. & Doering, A. (2012). *Integrating educational technology into teaching* (6th ed.). Boston: Pearson Education.

Roderick, M., & Camburn, E. (1999). Risk and recovery from course failure in the early years of high school. *American Education Journal* 36(2): 303–343.

Ruiz-de-Velasco, J. & Fix, M. (2000). *Overlooked and underserved: Immigrant Students in the U.S. secondary schools.* Washington, DC: Urban Institute.

Rumberger, R. (1995). Dropping out of middle school: A multilevel analysis of students and schools. *American Educational Research Journal* 32(2): 583–625.

Samson, J. & Collins, B. (2012). Preparing all teachers to meet the need of English Language Learners: Applying research to policy and practice. Center for American Progress. Retrieved from www.americanprogress.org.

Saunders, W. M. (1999). Improving literacy achievement for English learners in transitional bilingual programs. *Educational Research and Evaluation* 5, 345–381.

Saunders, W. M. & Goldenberg, C. (1999). The effects of comprehensive language arts/ Transition program on the literacy development of English learners. Retrieved From: http://www-gse.berkely.edu/research/crede.

Scarcella, R. (2003). *Accelerating academic English: A focus on the English language learners.* Oakland: Regents of the University of California.

Schleppergrell, M. (2002). *Developing advanced literacy in first and second languages: Meaning with power.* Mahwah, NJ: Lawrence Erlbaum Associates.

Schmitz, B. (1990). Transforming a course. Center for Instructional development and Research teaching and learning bulletin, 2(4), 1–2.

Schneider, B. & Lee, Y. (1990). A model for academic success: The school and home Environment of East Asian students. *Anthropology and Education Quarterly* 21: 358–377.

Shore, K. (2001). Success for ESL students. *Instructor*, 110(6): 30–32.

Shulman, L. & Sparks, D. (1992). Merging content knowledge and pedagogy: An interview with Lee Shulman. *Journal of Staff Development* 13(1): 14–16.

Slavin, R. E. & Calderon, M. (2001). *Effective programs for Latino students*. Mahwah, NJ: Lawrence Erlbaum.

Slavin, R. E. & Madden, N. (2001). *Effects of bilingual and English as a Second Language adaptations of success for all on the reading achievement of students acquiring English*. Mahwah, NJ: Lawrence Erlbaum.

Smith, G. (1966). *Communication and culture*. New York: Holt, Reinhart and Winston.

Smylie, M.A. (1988). The enhancement function of staff development: Organization and psychological antecedents to individual teacher change. *American Educational Research Journal* 25: 1–30.

Sosnowski, J. (2010). Statistics on how poverty affects children in schools. *Seattle Post-Intelligencer*. Retrieved from http://education.seattlepi.com/statistics-poverty-affects-Children-schools-3636.html.

Stein, R. (2004). Mexican and U.S. schools: A world apart. *The Term Paper* 3(1): 4.

Steinberg, L., Lin Blinde, P., & Chan, K. S. (1984). Dropping out among language minority youth. *Review of Educational Research* 54(1): 113–132.

Stephen, V. P., Varble, M. E., & Taitt, H. (1993). Instructional strategies for minority youth. *The Clearing House* 67: 116–120.

Taylor, P., Gonzalez-Barrera, A., Passel. J. & Hugo Lopez, M. (2012). An awakened giant: The Hispanic electorate is likely to double by 2030. Washington, DC: Pew Research Center.

Tharp, R. G. & Dalton, S. S. (2007). Orthodoxy, cultural compatibility and universals in education. *Comparative Education* 43(1): 53–70.

Tharp, R. G., Estrada, P., Dalton, S., & Yamauchi, L. (2000). *Teaching transformed: Achieving excellence, fairness, inclusion and harmony*. Boulder, CO: Westview.

Thayer, V. (1928). *The passing of the recitation*. Boston, MA: D.C. Heath.

Thompson, A. D., Schmidt, D. A., & Davis, N. E. (2003). Technology collaboratives for simultaneous renewal in teacher education. *Educational Technology Research and Development* 51(1): 124–129.

Thompson, D. (2001). What does it mean to call feminism "white and middle class"? In *Radical Feminism Today*. London: Sage.

Thompson, G. (2000). The real deal on bilingual education: Former language minority students discuss effective and ineffective instructional practices. *Educational Horizons* 78(2): 80–92.

Tomlinson, C. A. (1995). *How to differentiate instruction in mixed ability classrooms*. Alexandria, VA: Association for Supervision and Curriculum Development.

UNICEF. (2005). The state of the world's children. Retrieved from www.unicef.org/sowc05/english/.

U.S. Census Bureau. (2006). Poverty and health insurance coverage in the U.S. 2005: Current population reports. Retrieved from http://www.census.gov/prod/2006pubs/p60-231.pdf.

U.S. Department of Education. (2003). The conditions of education. Retrieved from www.nces.ed/gov/pubs2003/2003067.pdf.

U.S. Department of Education (2009). Trends in High School dropout and completion rates in the U.S., 1972-2009. National Center for Education Statistics. Retrieved from www.nces.ed.gov.

U.S. Department of Education. (2001). White House Initiative on American Indian and Alaska Native education. Retrieved from http://www.ed.gov/edblogs/whiaiane

U.S. Department of Education. (2006). The condition of education. National Center for Educational Statistics. Retrieved from nces.ed.gov.

Waxman, H. C. (1992). *Reversing the cycle of educational failure for students in at-risk school environments.* Newbury Park, CA: Sage.

Waxman, H. C., Padron, Y. N., & Knight, S. L. (1991). Risks associated with students limited Cognitive mastery. In W. C. Wang, M. C. Reynols, & H. J. Walberg (Eds). *Handbook of special education: Emerging programs,* vol. 4, 235–254. Oxford, England: Pergamon.

Webley, K. (2011) The achievement gap: Why Hispanic students are still behind. *Time.* U.S. Retrieved from http://content.time.com/time/nation/article.

Wells, G. & Chang-Wells, G. L. (1992). *Constructing knowledge together: Classrooms as centers of inquiry and literacy.* Portsmouth, NH: Heinemann.

Wiggins, R. A., Follo, E. J., & Eberly, W. B. (2007). The impact of a field immersion program on pre-service teachers' attitudes toward teaching in culturally diverse classrooms. *Teaching and Teacher Education* 23(5): 653.

Wilen, W. (1990). Forms and phrases of discussion. In W. Wilen (Ed.), *Teaching and Learning through discussion,* 3–24. Springfield, IL: Charles C. Thomas.

Wolf, D. (1988). *Reading reconsidered: Students, teachers and literature.* Princeton, NJ: Report to the College Board.

Wolk, S. (1998). *A democratic classroom.* Portsmouth, NH: Heinemann.

Yale University. (2014). Online teaching tools and resources. Retrieved from Yale Center for Language Study: http://cls.yale.edu/online-teaching-tools-resources.

About the Author

Michele Wages, PhD, is an instructional specialist serving on Title One campuses in the DFW area since 1993, including a bilingual campus with an 86-percent Hispanic student enrollment and a free and reduced lunch demographic of 96 percent. During her twenty-six-year career, she has been a classroom teacher, reading specialist, and language arts facilitator, and has provided staff development training for teachers. Dr. Wages received her bachelor's degree in social science and elementary education from the University of Michigan in Flint, her Master's in educational leadership from Texas Wesleyan University in Fort Worth, Texas, and her doctorate degree in curriculum and instruction from Capella University in Minneapolis, Minnesota. Her dissertation topic dealt with the effects of two types of bilingual programs on Hispanic student achievement in reading for grades 3–6. Michele lives in Texas with her two canine companions, Mr. Chips and Bailey, and enjoys her hobbies of gardening, refinishing antique furniture, and old muscle cars. She can be found on many sunny days behind the wheel of her 1967 Ford Mustang.

www.ingramcontent.com/pod-product-compliance
Lightning Source LLC
Chambersburg PA
CBHW050539270326
41926CB00015B/3305